Presented To:

_____

From:

_____

Date:

_____

THE
GLORY
WITHIN

THE GLORY WITHIN

*The Interior Life
and the Power of
Speaking in Tongues*

COREY RUSSELL

DESTINY IMAGE® PUBLISHERS, INC.

P.O. Box 310, Shippensburg, PA 17257-0310

"Promoting Inspired Lives."

This book and all other Destiny Image, Revival Press, MercyPlace, Fresh Bread, Destiny Image Fiction, and Treasure House books are available at Christian bookstores and distributors worldwide.

For a U.S. bookstore nearest you, call 1-800-722-6774.

For more information on foreign distributors, call 717-532-3040.

Reach us on the Internet: www.destinyimage.com.

ISBN 13 TP: 978-0-7684-4123-9

ISBN 13 Ebook: 978-0-7864-8838-8

For Worldwide Distribution, Printed in the U.S.A.

3 4 5 6 7 8 9 10 11 / 14 13 12

DEDICATION

To the apostle Paul, for speaking in tongues more than me.

ACKNOWLEDGMENTS

To Daniel Paravisini: Thank you for running with me and carrying this message with me over the last couple of years. I couldn't have done it without you.

To Jane Harris: Thank you for all of your tireless labor in compiling all of my notes, all of my thoughts, and being so patient with me throughout this entire process. You are a gift sent from God.

ENDORSEMENTS

Amazingly, the apostle Paul said, "I pray in tongues more than you all." Why? Why such a boast? There must have been some outrageous power and blessing in it for the greatest apostle to herald it. And if so there must be a great recovery of that ancient tongue of fire. My friend, Corey Russell, puts a compelling demand on that recovery in this book. It's not just words. For four years I've watched this man's prayer life, with many tongues in the Spirit leading to the mighty tongues of fire on his own life.

LOU ENGLE
Founder of The Call

The interior life is the most crucial and yet one of the most ignored aspects of the Christian life. If we as the Church are to fully shine in a dark world we can no longer ignore our interior life and must fully embrace the power of the Holy Spirit available to us. In *The Glory Within*, Corey Russell calls us to a deeper relationship with the Holy Spirit to unlock the strength available to all believers. God has raised up Corey as a voice to a generation and has anointed him to call the Church to experience the fullness of God. His teaching comes not from just theory but from a life lived in the secret place on a journey to discover the majesty and greatness of God.

BANNING LIEBSCHER
Jesus Culture Director

Corey Russell is a dear friend and close companion whose life I have closely observed for the last 11 years, and if there's anything that emanates from his life, it's friendship with Holy Spirit. He has consistently prioritized the size of his heart over the size of his ministry, and it is precisely this heart posture that will be entrusted with the nations in the coming days. This book contains more than good principles to aid your quiet times, but is a treasure given from a father on how to deeply know God. While reading this book, I was brought into times of deep communion, profound revelation, and a fresh hunger and urgency in my life to prioritize extended times of praying in the Holy Spirit. I wholeheartedly endorse this man of God and this book to you. I believe that it's these ancient paths of deep communion with Holy Spirit that will prepare this generation for the coming days of global glory and crisis.

ALLEN HOOD
Associate Director of International House of Prayer
President of International House of Prayer University

Corey Russell is a man of prayer. For years he has spent many hours a day praying and as he has sought the face of God, he has discovered the power of a specific form of prayer: speaking in tongues. The explosive power of praying in tongues is unlocked in each chapter of Corey's book. If you want to speak mysteries to God (see 1 Cor. 14:2) or need power in your inner man (see 1 Cor. 14:4), then this book is for you!

WESLEY AND STACEY CAMPBELL
Authors of *Praying the Bible: The Book of Prayers* and
Praying the Bible: The Pathway to Spirituality

CONTENTS

FOREWORD

by Mike Bickle

The greatest need of the hour in the Church is a call to the Body of Christ with a vision to go deep in God. We are living in the midst of a culture in the Church that has traded depth for width in regards to spirituality. We have defined "success" as the number of people who attend our services on Sunday, and the amount of money in our bank accounts, while our individual lives, marriages, and families are deteriorating all around us. A.W. Tozer's quote in *Knowledge of the Holy*, which was written 60 years ago, still rings true today: "We have lost our spirit of worship and our ability to withdraw inwardly to meet God in adoring silence."

Modern Christianity is simply not producing the kind of Christian who can appreciate or experience the life in the Spirit. The words, *"Be still, and know that I am God"* (Psalm 46:10a), mean next to nothing to the self-confident, bustling worshiper.

This loss of the concept of majesty has come just when the forces of religion are making dramatic gains and the churches are more prosperous than at any time within the past several hundred years. But the alarming thing is that our gains are mostly external and our losses wholly internal. And since it is the quality of our religion that is affected by internal conditions, it may be that our supposed gains are but losses spread over a wider field.

It's in the midst of days like these that God raises up voices that call the Church back to her first love of intimacy with God and focus on the interior life so that once again, our lives would emanate the life of Christ. Corey Russell is one of these voices. Corey has been on the senior leadership team at IHOP (International House of Prayer) for the last 11 years. His messages on the knowledge of God and intimacy with God carry authority and clarity.

They are challenging and provoking to all who hear him. His leadership in the house of prayer, in our school, at our conferences, and abroad continually imparts and equips all who hear him in the call to go deep in God.

His book, *The Glory Within: The Interior Life and the Power of Speaking in Tongues*, will inspire many to grow in their intimacy with Jesus. In this book, Corey lays forth the glorious reality of the new birth, the indwelling Spirit, and then takes us on the journey of accessing the life of the Spirit within. His writing lays out the benefits of praying in the spirit. It gives helpful insight, and is very practical. I believe that the people who take this book and apply these realities will look back at it as a transformational and life-altering book that contributed to their spiritual lives. This subject has impacted my life and ministry over the years. I believe it will do the same for those who give themselves to it.

MIKE BICKLE
Founder, International House of Prayer
Kansas City, Missouri

Chapter 1

Born of God

Fifteen years have now passed since the encounter that changed my life, but I remember it vividly. I was born and raised in a small town in Northwest Arkansas. My family was loving and godly, and we attended church every Sunday. In my mind, however, there was no difference between attending church on Sunday and attending football practice on Monday; it was just what you were supposed to do on that particular day.

I did not have a personal and real salvation experience in those early days. Therefore, when I was presented with opportunities to indulge in drugs, alcohol, and relationships at the age of 13, I said yes. (I knew I was supposed to "Just Say No," but a red ribbon that I pinned to my shirt once a year did not motivate me to actually say no.) I partied through high school, and the partying increased in college. Toward the end of my freshmen year at college, my mother came to visit me. It broke her heart to see the effects of my lifestyle: I had lost quite a bit of weight, my eyes were sunken, and my zest for life was quickly disappearing. She begged me to come home for the summer in the hopes that she could get some weight back on me and distance me from the party scene.

That summer, while at home, I received my first DWI (driving while intoxicated) ticket. I couldn't afford to go back to my university so I decided to remain at home and attend the local community college. The one bright spot in all of this was that one of my best friends, Zach, had a really great local drug hookup. We decided to get an apartment and take the partying to the next level. At this time, we began doing drugs that would keep us up for five days straight.

This continued until November 1996. That month we came off of a drug binge—and Zach had changed. After that binge, he behaved differently, as though part of him was lost. For the next four months, Zach hardly spoke to anyone and seemed to stare at people as though he was seeing things that others could not. This odd behavior continued up until February 1, 1997. After partying at the University of Arkansas, a friend and I decided to pick up Zach and hang out. When I pulled up in front of the house and got out of the car, I heard someone screaming. Suddenly, Zach burst through the front door, running full speed at me and screaming, "Corey, it's Heaven or hell! Make a decision!" He screamed this over and over until we were face-to-face. I tried to talk to him, but he only repeated that phrase. Finally I grabbed my other friend and left.

Later we learned what had happened. Zach came from a very intense home, and his mother was what I would call an "old time" intercessor; she always seemed to be awake, no matter the time of day or night, wrapped in a blanket, praying in tongues, and anointing everyone and everything with oil. The last week of January she attended a conference and responded to an altar call for parents: Come and get your children! She rushed forward to cry out for breakthrough, and the Lord promised her that within the week her son would be saved. On that February day, Zach had just completed three days of deliverance with his mother. During those three days, she prayed over him, read the Bible over him, and took authority over any spirits that manifested. After those three days, Zach was freed from addiction and reconnected with the faith of his youth.

As the news of Zach's salvation spread, I became more and more angry. I had put up with months of his odd and disturbing behavior; now I felt betrayed because he had chosen to be "born again." In my opinion, Christians were the most boring people on the face of the Earth, and from what I had witnessed, most of them seemed to enjoy their Tuesday night sitcoms more than they enjoyed the presence of the Lord on Sundays. I couldn't believe that Zach was a Christian! It was a very dark time for me.

Two weeks later, Zach showed up at my community college and took me out to lunch. Over the meal, he explained what had happened to him during the four months following our November drug binge. The spirit realm had been opened to him and he had seen demons controlling people. He was tormented as he witnessed these dark spirits influencing those around him, including me. The experience culminated at a late-night house party. In the midst of the party, he heard the voice of the Lord say, "Satan is raising up an army, but I am raising up an army too, and I am calling you out tonight." After sharing this, he began to press me, saying, "Corey, you need to make a decision now, or you will go to hell."

I told him to shut up and take me back to school. (I had just received my second DWI ticket and my license was suspended.) We drove the five minutes back to the community college in complete silence; my heart was incredibly hard, and I wanted nothing to do with Christianity. As we pulled into the parking lot, I suddenly felt a presence enter the van. I did not know it at the time, but it was the Holy Spirit. I began to shake violently, as though I were having a seizure. Demons were manifesting, and for the first time, I saw the battle between light and darkness raging in my soul.

Zach began to pray, and then he shouted, "In the name of Jesus, I bind the antichrist spirit!" Immediately, I felt as though a rope had closed around my neck, and I began to choke. I couldn't breathe, but I knew that I had to say the name of Jesus. In that moment, all my petty arguments against Christianity vanished. Each time I tried to say, "Jesus," the choke hold tightened, but finally, after wrestling for a while, I took a deep breath and screamed at the top of my lungs, "Jesus!" Immediately, the choking sensation vanished. Zach leapt out of the van and began to dance around and yell. I just kept repeating, "I've got air; I've got air." It literally felt as though new breath had entered me. After a few minutes, I heard a voice within me telling me to get out of the van and kneel on the ground. Then I heard, clearly and powerfully, "Give Me your life." I immediately jumped out of the van and knelt on that college parking lot. As students passed on their way to and from class, I began to violently scream, "Jesus, I give You my life! I'm Yours!"

In that moment—on Tuesday, February 18, 1997—the power of my years of addiction to alcohol, drugs, and perversion was broken, and I knew that I had crossed over from death to life. Zach and I drove home, and I walked through the front door, fell into my mother's lap, and cried as I repeated again and again, "Mom, I got saved today." I sat on our front porch swing later that day, looking at the grass and the trees and feeling overwhelmed by how green they were. It was as though I had never seen nature before—as though I had been blind for 20 years and was now seeing for the first time.

When I cried out to Jesus, something greater than a simple change of heart occurred; I knew that I had been transformed. Although the change was not external or physical, I felt an explosion of life and power deep within the core of my being—and 15 years later I still feel the reverberations of that initial transformation. Immediately, years of addiction and bondage were broken; the reality of the existence of God and eternity began to fill my thoughts and inform my decisions. This had never been the case before, but now God was intensely real to me.

Paul states that *"if anyone is in Christ, he is a new creation; old things have passed away; behold, all things have become new"* (2 Cor. 5:17). The apostle did not use these words lightly; he understood that when we are saved, a powerful act of creation occurs within us. Just as Adam was entirely new when the breath of God entered him and he opened his eyes for the first time, so we are entirely new when we enter into Christ. The same God who created light through the power of His voice has created life within us:

> *For it is the God who commanded light to shine out of darkness, who has shone in our hearts to give the light of the knowledge of the glory of God in the face of Jesus Christ* (2 Corinthians 4:6).

We must rediscover this newness of life in our generation; we must know in an intensely real way that we who are born again have undergone a glorious transformation and that God literally lives within us. Only then will we be able to live effectively and victoriously.

John 3

What exactly happened to me that February day as I knelt in the college parking lot? How could I be completely blind to the reality of God at one moment and then find myself on my knees crying out at the top of my lungs to Jesus in the next? I'm convinced that the answer to these questions will birth a great revival in the Church worldwide. According to the language of the Bible, I was "born again" in that parking lot—but what does that even mean? I certainly didn't know what it meant at the time; all I knew was that after that day, everything changed. While I used to feel dead in the midst of day-to-day life, suddenly I felt truly alive. I experienced a radical internal revolution, and it changed my entire nature from within.

This subject of being "born again" confronted Nicodemus when he sought to convince Jesus to align with the religious leadership in Jerusalem. Jesus cut right to the point, saying in essence: "You and the Pharisees think you know who I am, but you must undergo a radical rebirth to understand and agree with who I truly am." *"Jesus answered and said to him, 'Most assuredly, I say to you, unless one is born again, he cannot see the kingdom of God'"* (John 3:3).

As a Pharisee, the entirety of Nicodemus' life was focused around the Kingdom of God, yet Jesus told this brilliant Jewish scholar that he would blindly miss the point of his existence if he was not radically recreated and reborn. Famously, the phrase *born again* caught Nicodemus off guard and confused him. *"Nicodemus said to Him, 'How can a man be born when he is old? Can he enter a second time into his mother's womb and be born?'"* (John 3:4). Nicodemus wrestled with the implications of Jesus' statement in the natural realm. In His response, however, Jesus made it clear that He was not primarily referring to the natural realm.

> *Jesus answered, "Most assuredly, I say to you, unless*
> *one is born of water and the Spirit, he cannot enter*
> *the kingdom of God. That which is born of the flesh*

is flesh, and that which is born of the Spirit is spirit"
(John 3:5-6).

Jesus used the natural to establish the supernatural; He took the familiar and used it to create a bridge to the unfamiliar. It was and is the kindness of God to use analogies and parables to usher us into the deeper things of the Spirit. Then Jesus offered Nicodemus a new analogy:

> *Do not marvel that I said to you, "You must be born again." The wind blows where it wishes, and you hear the sound of it, but cannot tell where it comes from and where it goes. So is everyone who is born of the Spirit* (John 3:7-8).

Just as we can feel and discern the presence of the wind without knowing where it comes from, so it is with those born of the Spirit: They feel and discern the reality of their new birth and the presence of the Spirit, but they are unable to explain it or to show where it came from. The things of the Spirit can only be known through the revelation of the Holy Spirit (see 1 Cor. 2:13-16).

This is why Jesus exclaimed that Nicodemus would never understand heavenly realities. Jesus ended the discussion with just such a reality:

> *If I have told you earthly things and you do not believe, how will you believe if I tell you heavenly things? No one has ascended to heaven but He who came down from heaven, that is, the Son of Man who is in heaven* (John 3:12-13).

What a statement: as He stood before Nicodemus, *Jesus boldly declared that He was in Heaven, by the Spirit, at that moment.* Nicodemus must have thought, *You are not in Heaven; You are clearly here in front of me*, to which Jesus might have replied, with a smile, "That is what you think."

This book is about the glorious reality of God dwelling in human vessels. From this revelation, we are called to actively access the life that has been given to us. We have all been guilty of treating phrases such as *born again, new creation,* and *saved* with over-familiarity. Many of us have relegated these realities to an altar call that we went forward for years ago: "Praise God, now I am going to Heaven." Because we do not understand what happened at that altar call, we have forfeited the glorious inheritance that is now available to us by the indwelling Holy Spirit. We may know all of the Christian buzzwords and phrases, but we are trapped in cycles of depression, fear, addiction, and shame, and we cannot seem to save our marriages or our families. We confess that we have all things in Christ Jesus, yet this truth seems so far from our everyday lives. Do we really understand that the power to bring breakthrough in our hearts and transformation in our lives dwells inside of us?

BORN OF GOD

In many of his New Testament writings, the apostle John expounds on this glorious reality of being "born of God." He wrote his Gospel and epistles as an old man nearing the end of his life, and with fatherly care he continually reminded his young followers what it meant to be "born of God." He didn't see this subject as something that a person moves on from; he understood it as the foundation to everything in the Christian life.

John opens his Gospel with a reference to this new birth.

> *Yet to all who received Him, to those who believed in His name, He gave the right to become children of God—children born not of natural descent, nor of*

human decision or a husband's will, but born of God (John 1:12-13 NIV).

Take a moment and consider the phrase *born of God*. Please put the book down and meditate on those words. We have all experienced birth in our natural families. Each of us possesses the genes and traits of our parents. Of course, when a child is first born, we do not see the full resemblance; the fullness of the genetic inheritance on the inside is not yet displayed. But as time passes and the child grows, he or she begins to bear a greater resemblance to the parents. In some instances, the child looks like the father—having his eyes, his ears, his nose, his hair color, his body type, or even his personality. This is because the father's genes are alive within the child.

In the same way that a child is birthed into a natural family and contains the DNA and characteristics of the parents, so we who are born of God have been birthed into the spiritual reality of the Kingdom and contain the DNA of God. The fullness of this reality does not manifest right away, but as we engage the life of God within us, it grows until eventually we begin to look like Him and walk like Him. First John 3:9 declares that the very seed of God remains in us. This seed is powerful because it contains the fullness of God.[1] The day that we said yes to Jesus, God placed His seed within us and birthed into our spirits His very own Spirit. I love to quietly repeat this phrase to myself: "I am born of God." I have the DNA of God within me; His very life, His very mind, His heart, His longings, and His dreams live within me and invite me to partake of them.

"Whoever has been born of God does not sin, for His seed remains in him; and he cannot sin, because he has been born of God" (1 John 3:9). This verse can be confusing at first glance. John is not claiming that those who are born again walk in sinless perfection. Earlier in the first chapter, he stated that if we say we have no

sin, then we make God a liar. Here in chapter 3, John is saying that *anyone who is born of God will be an unsuccessful sinner.* The person who has truly been born of God is not comfortable with habitual sin that continues for any length of time. Such people cannot sin without the Holy Spirit convicting them, challenging them, and creating remorse within them. They cannot get away from the need for repentance!

I remember an incident that occurred about two months after I was saved. I crossed some boundaries with a woman I was seeing at the time—something I had done before without remorse. Now, however, the spirit of conviction rested heavily on me. What I had once done without the slightest twinge of conscience now had me weeping. I began to understand that my life truly was no longer my own and that *Someone* now lived inside of me who did not like what I was doing! John does not claim that believers won't sin, but he does state that we will never be happy or successful sinners.

"You are of God, little children, and have overcome them, because He who is in you is greater than he who is in the world" (1 John 4:4). *"For whatever is born of God overcomes the world. And this is the victory that has overcome the world—our faith"* (1 John 5:4). Here is another characteristic of those who have experienced the new birth: Whoever is born of God overcomes the world. There is something alive within every believer that has the ability to stand firm despite the resistance of the world, the flesh, and the devil. Just as Jesus overcame in His life, so we now overcome through His life in us. Overcoming is not floating over every hardship and trial.

Instead, overcoming is possessing life inside of us that enables us to persevere despite external circumstances. It is the ability, the perseverance, the grace, and the endurance to stay steady through every trial (see Heb. 11). The world, the spirit of this age, and spirits of darkness constantly oppress unbelievers, but we have something within us that resists oppression and allows us to walk in victory. God has also given us the power to move into the offensive (versus the defensive) in the face of oppression and negative circumstances. We can actually take ground in the spirit and thereby overcome external circumstances, too.

CHRIST IN YOU

Jesus told His disciples that He would not leave them alone, but that they would see Him and that He would dwell in them, giving them the power to overcome. This is the great mystery of the Christian life that Paul reveals in his letter to the Colossian church: *"Christ in you, the hope of glory"* (Col. 1:27b). Paul boldly declares that the mystery seen by the prophets of old, the mystery hidden in God from before the foundation of the world, was that Gentiles would become the dwelling place of Christ Himself. For those of us who have surrendered our lives to Jesus, He is in us right now, and we are not alone. "Christ in you"—His life, His presence, His resources, His power, His wisdom, and His love reside within us right now. When we receive by faith His life within us, we are empowered to walk as He walks, think as He thinks, and live as He lives.

First Corinthians says that *"he who is joined to the Lord is one spirit with Him"* (1 Cor. 6:17). I like to picture a giant umbilical cord connecting me to Jesus as He sits at the right hand of God. What do umbilical cords do? They release nutrients and food to the child. They are the life source. No matter where we go or what we do, we are connected with Christ by a giant, invisible umbilical cord. All of the life and resources of Jesus are available to us. It is critical that we understand that we are joined to Christ. We are not next to Him; we are one with Him. And He is in us. Right now we have the ability to feel what Jesus is feeling, see what He is seeing, know what He is thinking, and pray what He is praying. I pray this often: "Jesus, give me Your prayers. What are You feeling and thinking and praying?"

The indwelling life of the Holy Spirit was the subject matter that consumed Jesus when He was preparing to head to the cross. His last discourse recorded in the Gospel of John was on the person and work of the Holy Spirit. Jesus did not want to leave His disciples without grounding them in an understanding of the Holy Spirit! In John 13–16, Jesus told the disciples, "You are not alone." He was strengthening these young men, and comforting their hearts over His departure in the face of a religious system and a Roman government that wanted to kill them. They had been led and sheltered by Him for three and a half years, and now they were about to experience intense persecution on their own. Instead of placing weapons in their hands, He introduced them to a *Person*.

This Person is Himself, yet distinct as the third person of the Trinity, the Holy Spirit. Jesus spent so much time that evening introducing them to the Holy Spirit, to His ministry and how they would relate to Him. One of the main functions of Jesus' coming was the sending of the Holy Spirit. John the Baptist's greatest revelation of Jesus was that Jesus was Jesus the Baptist, the One who would baptize with the Holy Spirit and fire.

Jesus strengthened their hearts as His departure neared by sharing that, though He had been with them in the flesh, now He would be with them in the Spirit. They would no longer be limited in their interactions with Him by time and distance, because He was going to live inside of them. Although the world would not be able to receive Him—for it had not known Him and soon would not see Him—the disciples would know and see Him through fellowship with the Holy Spirit. They would not be orphans, for the Holy Spirit would father them, teach them, and bring to their remembrance everything that Jesus had taught and said. I can imagine Jesus looking at Peter and Thomas and saying, "Guys, in the coming years, when you are in prison and are being persecuted for your faith, know that you are not alone. I am in you, and My very life and presence will comfort and strengthen you. You can speak with Me, commune with Me, and fellowship with Me anytime and anywhere."

This is why Jesus told the disciples that it was actually to their *advantage* that He leave and send the Holy Spirit. We need to understand that it is better for us now than if we had been disciples when Jesus walked the Earth. Jesus in the flesh was confined in His interactions by space and time. Yet through the Holy Spirit, God can dwell in and commune with every believer, and we each as individuals have unlimited access to His life. This reality has been the desire of God from the beginning. We were made to commune with God, spirit-to-Spirit.

However, we will not experience this reality unless we become well acquainted with the Holy Spirit and engage Him in an intimate way. Is the Holy Spirit our best friend? Do we talk to Him, confide in Him, listen to Him, and hang out with Him? If we want more of God, if we want to experience the fullness of salvation, then we must develop deep fellowship with the Holy Spirit.

ENDNOTE

1. Although God places His fullness within us, most believers access very little of it. For them, this fullness remains potential rather than actual and experiential.

Chapter 2

MADE FOR COMMUNION

In his book *I Believe in Visions*, Kenneth Hagin shares an encounter he had during a difficult season. He was in the hospital with an injured arm, and one night as he lay in his bed, he heard someone coming down the hallway toward him. When the door opened, Jesus walked into his hospital room. For over an hour, the Lord sat with him and spoke about the ministry of angels, the office of the prophet, the purpose of visions and encounters, and the prophetic ministry. It was an intense time of revelation and communion. Right before He left, Jesus told Hagin that He would not guide him in his day-to-day life by the supernatural ministry of the prophetic. Instead, He said that Hagin would be led, as all believers are, by the inward witness of the Holy Spirit. "If you will learn to follow this inward witness, I will help you in all the affairs of your life."[1]

When we read a story like this, many of us imagine that we would feel disappointed if Jesus told us He would not visit us again in an open vision or encounter, but instead would relate to us by the Spirit within. However, through this encounter, Jesus revealed to Hagin (and to us) that there is no qualitative difference between open visions and encounters and the life of the Holy Spirit living on the inside of us. That still, small voice of the Spirit of God within is as real and powerful as the thunders of His voice. It's when we understand this that we come to rest and begin to engage Him, knowing that He will speak with us. We were made for deep intimacy and deep revelation of the things of God. This is our inheritance!

SPIRIT, SOUL, AND BODY

"...May your whole spirit, soul and body be preserved blameless..." (1 Thess. 5:23). God designed humanity as an intricate, three-part reality: body, soul, and spirit. In the same way, God formed the tabernacle with an outer court, an inner court, and the holy of holies. God has designed us with an outer court (our body), an inner court (our personality or soul—the mind, will, and emotions), and a holy of holies (our spirit person). It is in our spirits that God comes to take up residence at the new birth. The very life of God is infused into us, and we receive this new nature deep within our spirits.

We are spirits who have souls and live in bodies. Who we really are is not what can be seen externally, but who we are deep within. Watchman Nee describes humanity's three-part nature this way: "God dwells in the spirit, the self dwells in the soul, and the senses dwell in the body."[2] God is Spirit (see John 4:24), and humanity needed to be spirit as well in order to experience and contain His presence. The soul is defined as our mind, will, and emotions. It is the source of our unique identity and our free will, and it encompasses our thoughts, desires, and personality. These faculties are what enable us to relate to God emotionally, intellectually, and by choice. In all of creation, only humanity possesses the ability to relate to God in this way. Finally, the body enables us to relate to the physical world around us. Through our senses we understand creation, and through our physical actions we impact it.

In salvation, God addresses all three parts of our nature. Our spirits are saved when we receive Jesus as our Lord and Savior. This is what the Bible calls justification. Jesus cleanses us from our sins and justifies us in the presence of God. At that point we begin the process of sanctification. This is the saving of our souls, which includes our thought life, emotional chemistry, and desires. As we position our hearts, God begins to transform our souls and set them apart for Him and Him alone. Ultimately, salvation involves the saving of our bodies, which will occur at the second coming of the Lord, when the dead are raised and receive resurrected, glorified bodies. This statement is true for every Christian: I have been saved, I am being saved, and I am going to be saved.

Let's take a little more time to look at the intricate design of our spirit, soul, and body. God's great dilemma is creating a structure that can handle His glory and not be destroyed by it. Every time we see God in temples, the temples are barely holding up because of the weight of His glory. It was in the creation of human bodies that God solved this dilemma. God designed us as creatures that would be able to contain His very life within us and we would not blow up. You need to be thanking God every day that there isn't smoke coming out of your ears! So many believers spend the majority of their lives despising their bodies, hating the very design of their frame, and it's our bodies that have been fearfully and wonderfully made to contain the glory of God. In First Corinthians 6:13b, Paul makes this incredible statement concerning our bodies when calling them out of immorality: *"Now the body is not for sexual immorality but for the Lord, and the Lord for the body."* Paul states earlier that in the same way that food and the stomach are intricately connected, so is our body and the Lord. The two were designed for one another, and it's when we understand this connection that we begin to love what He loves. Even many sicknesses and diseases are related to self-hatred of our bodies.

It's when we understand the relationship between our spirits, souls, and bodies that the presence of Christ is released in us, through us, and all around us. This is the divine order. Our souls and our bodies are meant to exist in submission to our spirits, and our spirits in turn are meant to be led by the Spirit of God. *Everything in our lives is meant to flow from our spirit-to-Spirit communion with God—we were designed for this very purpose.* We were made to relate to God.

MADE FOR COMMUNION

Then God said, "Let Us make man in Our image, according to Our likeness; let them have dominion over the fish of the sea, over the birds of the air, and over the cattle, over all the earth and over every creeping thing that creeps on the earth" (Genesis 1:26).

In Genesis 1 we see God unveiling His creation in an ascending order of glory. Ten consecutive times He created an original living creature and then a counterpart. This divine pattern of creation was clearly established. Each counterpart was created according to the kind (or in the likeness) of the original. God's purpose was to bring the two counterparts together in union in order to generate life.

On the sixth day, however, God did something different. Instead of creating an original and then a likeness according to its kind, God created a likeness alone, for the Original already existed. This last creation was designed as a counterpart

36

to the pre-existent, uncreated second Person of the Trinity; Adam and Eve were created for union with Jesus. This was the divine purpose behind the creation of humanity. God desired to unite Himself with a part of His creation and, through that union, release the flow of divine life to the rest of the created order. We were made to connect with God, Spirit-to-spirit, and then release supernatural life in the natural realm. The three-part nature of humanity and the design of the human spirit is God's statement of His desire for intimacy. We were made in the image of God to commune with and relate to Him. We have the capacity to relate to the infinite, uncreated God. No other creatures, not even the angels, have this capacity or this privilege. Deep within, humanity was designed to be the habitation of the Spirit of God.

From man's standpoint the most tragic loss suffered in the Fall was the vacating of this inner sanctum by the Spirit of God. At the far-in hidden center of man's being is a bush fitted to be the dwelling place of the Triune God. There God planned to rest and glow with moral and spiritual fire. Man by his sin forfeited this indescribably wonderful privilege and must now dwell there alone. For so intimately private is the place that no creature can intrude; no one can enter but Christ; and He will enter only by the invitation of faith.[3]

This is why the fall was so devastating. I believe we often do not feel the weight of what really happened when sin entered the hearts of Adam and Eve. The Life that dwelt deep within them suddenly left, and they were alone. This resulted in a deep chasm between two realms that had previously been united. The fall was a divorce: God and humanity were separated when the human spirit was vacated from the life of God. There was no longer a place within humanity for God to dwell. Heaven and Earth were separated too, and the whole cosmos was thrown into disarray as the image-bearers lost connection with God.

The story did not end there, however. One of the central verses when it comes to understanding redemptive history is found in Ephesians:

> *That in the dispensation of the fullness of the times*
> *He might gather together in one all things in Christ,*
> *both which are in heaven and which are on earth—in*
> *Him* (Ephesians 1:10).

God is working to reunite all of creation through and in Christ. The fullness of redemption is about marriage between God and people, between Heaven and Earth; it's about individuals and the Earth itself becoming the dwelling place of God once more.

This desire within the heart of God for communion and a dwelling place is the thrust behind redemptive history. In Genesis 3:15, God promised to bring forth a Seed that would crush the head of the serpent and restore people to the glory of their original design. God did not sit idly by as humanity tumbled into the depths of depravity. Instead, through the prophecy of the Seed, He revealed the means by which He would redeem humanity and reunite Heaven and Earth through the release of the Kingdom. The coming of the Seed is the answer to the longing in God's heart for communion and a dwelling place, and it is the promise that drives the Old Testament narrative. Through His dealings with Abraham, Moses, David, and the nation of Israel, God gave humanity the storyline that culminated in the One who would pay for our sins and restore our communion with God.

In the fullness of time, God sent His Son to the planet as the last Adam to restore all that was lost in the Garden. When God could not find a sinless person who could reconcile God and humanity, God became that Man. Jesus took on our flesh, lived the perfect life for us, and died our death. When all other ways failed and when all people fell short, God offered His Son as a sacrifice, thus opening the way for God and humanity to become one again.

> *Therefore, as through one man's offense judgment came to all men, resulting in condemnation, even so through one Man's righteous act the free gift came to all men, resulting in justification of life* (Romans 5:18).

The free gift is the life of Christ within us, which justifies us in the presence of God. When Jesus broke the power of sin and death on the third day, He ascended into Heaven and poured out His very Spirit. On the day of Pentecost, humanity became the habitation of God once again.

THE CALL TO FELLOWSHIP

So here are the facts: If we have surrendered our lives to Jesus Christ and made Him our Lord and Savior, then right now—whether we feel it or not, whether our circumstances are good or bad, whether our relationships are positive or negative—we have the very Spirit of God dwelling deep within our spirits. The Spirit who raised Jesus from the dead, the God of Genesis 1 who spoke the universe into existence, lives in us. Jesus Christ now dwells within all believers, regardless of their ethnicity, their gender, their background, or their struggles. And not only is Christ in us, but more than that, we are in Him. Our lives are hidden in Christ, and right now, in the presence of God, we are as clean as Jesus is clean, and we are as close to the Father as Jesus is close to the Father. We are blessed with every spiritual blessing in the heavenly places *in Christ* (see Eph. 1:3). We are one spirit with Him, which means that His thoughts, His desires, His plans, and His life are now ours.

Few believers truly understand what now dwells within them. We have treasures living inside of us—all the riches and glory and strength of God Himself deposited within our spirits (see Eph. 3:16), and so many of us don't have a clue. I say this often: *We have a billion dollars in our bellies, yet most of us live on 20 cents a day.* The great preacher and revivalist Leonard Ravenhill recounted a conversation he had with theologian A.W. Tozer concerning this reality:

> I think again of a statement A. W. Tozer made to me once. He said, "Len, you know, we'll hardly get our feet out of time into eternity that we'll bow our heads in shame and humiliation. We'll gaze on eternity and say, 'Look at all the riches there were in Jesus Christ, and I've come to the Judgment Seat almost a pauper.'" For God had not only given us Jesus Christ—He has with Him freely given us all things (see Rom. 8:32).[4]

We're living as starving beggars, and we don't even know it. We spend millions of dollars on counseling and self-help, yet we see so little fruit in our lives. We wear ourselves out with religious activity, and still we find ourselves trapped in cycles of fear, depression, rejection, and self-hatred. As a result, we turn to comfort zones of overindulgence found in alcohol, entertainment, food, ungodly relationships—all of this to run from the poverty of our souls.

At some point, each of us has to take an honest look at our lives and ask: Where is the breakdown? If I have been *given* the fullness of the life of God, why don't I *experience* it? If I have everything in Christ, why do I walk in so little love and joy and peace? Where is the breakdown? Hopefully by now the revelation of all that we have been given in Christ is creating a deeper hunger in our spirits and a prayer is growing inside of us: *How can I access the life of God in me? How can I begin to see the Holy Spirit break out of my spirit and transform every area of my life—body, soul, and spirit?*

This question is what John 15 is all about. In John 15, Jesus states that He is the Vine and we are the branches. Think about the analogy Jesus used. The vine contains the life source—it contains the sap—and the vine also contains the branches. In the same way that the branches are connected to the vine, we are in Christ. We are in the vine, yet Jesus still gives us this command as branches. He calls us to abide in the vine. This means that, even though we are already in Christ, *we must, through an act of our own will, consciously and deliberately draw on the sap of the life of God within us.* We must draw on the sap, the life source, the power that has been placed within us through deliberately fellowshipping and communing with the Holy Spirit.

Many of us think that when it comes to our transformation, God will do everything and we don't have a part to play. The truth, though, is that God has a part and we have a part. We cannot do God's part, and God will not do our part. This is a major stumbling block on the road to maturity and transformation. We are all guilty of passivity—so many of us sit around wishing that our lives were different while refusing to go on the treasure hunt to discover what we've been given and how to access it. The author of Hebrews states that God rewards those who diligently seek Him, which means this: If we answer the call to actively fellowship with God, then we will see the power and life of the Holy Spirit break out of our spirits and spread like a wildfire, transforming every area of our lives.

Now that we've looked at what we possess in Christ, felt the sting of the gap between what we possess and what we experience, and heard the call to deliberately access what we have been given through fellowshipping with the Holy Spirit, the question remains: *How* do we fellowship with the Holy Spirit? How do we access the glorious riches dwelling deep within us? This question haunted me for years, but as I searched the Word of God, I found a clear roadmap. The way to access the life of God is very simple, so simple that few actually practice it. I want to highlight the three specific practices that I discovered in my journey of fellowshipping with the Holy Spirit. All three have been a significant source of life and breakthrough, but I will focus specifically on the third. The first is meditation on the Word of God, the second is dialogue with the Holy Spirit, and the third is praying in tongues.

FELLOWSHIP THROUGH MEDITATION

In John 15:7-8, Jesus told the disciples that one of the most practical ways to draw on the life of the Vine is to abide in His words:

> *If you abide in Me, and My words abide in you, you will ask what you desire, and it shall be done for you. By this My Father is glorified, that you bear much fruit; so you will be My disciples.*

When we immerse ourselves in His words, we are actually drawing on the life of God. In John 6, Jesus said that His words are spirit and life. If we want to experience the life of the Spirit then we need to become intimate with His words, because the Word of God and the Holy Spirit are one.

Because of this reality, we cannot read the Word of God the way that we read other books. It is not a history book, a biography, or a novel; it is the communicated life of God. We need a radical shift in our approach to the Word of God. If we are honest, most of us would say that the Bible is a place of frustration rather than a place of encounter. The thing that is supposed to give us life often leads to drudgery, condemnation, and boredom. I am convinced that this is because of the approach we take.

Many of us read the Bible the same way that we crammed the night before a test in high school: we read quickly for information and then think that, because we did the assignment, we know the material. Our goal shouldn't only be to read through the Bible in a year; our goal should be to encounter God and experience transformation. So many Christians are quick to say, "I know that verse," but I like to ask the question, "Does that verse know you? Is it alive in your spirit?"

In John 5, Jesus highlighted the fact that knowing Scripture was not enough when He spoke to the Pharisees:

> *You search the Scriptures, for in them you think you have eternal life; and these are they which testify of Me. But you are not willing to come to Me that you may have life* (John 5:39-40).

In other words, Jesus said, "I love that you love the Scriptures, but you need to understand that they are supposed to lead you to encounter with Me." The Pharisees followed the Word and studied the Word, but they were unwilling to allow the Word made flesh to confront and humble them. It is sobering to think that these men who knew the most about the Messiah actually killed the Messiah.

It is crucial that we take the approach of Mary of Bethany, who sat at the feet of Jesus in Luke 10, listening to His words. We cannot stand over the Word of God; the Word must stand over us. We must come to Jesus with reverence and allow His words to transform us, wash us, and impart the life of God. This approach is one of humility and submission, where we become listeners at His feet, slowly reading and turning the Word into prayers. Hans

Urs von Balthasar, the great Swiss theologian, describes meditation and prayer in this way:

> [F]irstly, prayer is a conversation between God and the soul, and secondly, a particular language is spoken: God's language. Prayer is dialogue, not man's monologue before God.... All of a sudden we just know: prayer is a conversation in which God's word has the initiative and we, for the moment, can be nothing more than listeners. The essential thing is for us to hear God's word and discover from it how to respond to him.[5]

This is how I approach my times of meditation.

When I speak of meditation, I'm speaking of the slow, repetitious reading and praying of the Word of God. It is important to read slowly and linger over verses. *We cannot read just for information; we must also read for impartation.* Every word is fragrant and filled with the Holy Spirit; every phrase in the Bible is anointed; every syllable is packed with revelation, and God is waiting for someone to come and unpack it. We want to catch the anointing as we read.

In Psalm 1 the psalmist says, "Blessed is the man who meditates on your law day and night" (see Ps. 1:1-2). That word *meditate* means "to ponder by speaking to one's self." I actually read the verse out loud, and I repeat the phrases that resonate with my spirit. There is power in the spoken Word of God: His words called light into existence, and they will fill us with light as we speak them over ourselves. Then I turn the verse into questions and prayers—this is pondering. The greatest secret I have found to unlocking the revelation and anointing of Scripture is asking questions. Who? Why? Where? When? These questions will set our souls on fire and open up doors of revelation in the Word.

Finally, I visualize what I am reading, and I pray in the Spirit. Our minds are easily distracted, and we will end up frustrated if we try to stop their activity. Instead, we can channel the busyness of our minds by visualizing what we are reading and by bringing our minds under the leadership of the Holy Spirit as we read the Word.

This, then, is what I do when I meditate: 1) read slowly, 2) repeat phrases, 3) turn the phrases into questions and prayers, 4) visualize, and 5) pray in the Spirit. What does this look like? Take for example John 5:19, where Jesus says, *"Most assuredly, I say to you, the Son can do nothing of Himself, but what He sees the Father do; for whatever He does, the Son also does in like manner."* I will read this slowly several times, and then I will ask: "Whatever You see the Father doing—what did You see? How did You see the Father? Did You see with Your natural eyes? Your spiritual eyes? What is the Father doing? You say that the Father is working." As I ask these questions, I will visualize Jesus talking to the Father. "How did You talk to Him?" Then I will begin to pray the phrases: "I want to see what You're doing, Father. I want to see You like Jesus saw You. I want to do what You are doing and live as Jesus lived." Finally, I will pray in the Spirit. Meditating in this way involves all of our faculties in exploring and unpacking the life and revelation contained in Scripture and our souls and our senses will be saturated with the Word of God as a result.[6]

FELLOWSHIP THROUGH DIALOGUE

"The grace of the Lord Jesus Christ, and the love of God, and the fellowship of the Holy Spirit, be with you all" (2 Cor. 13:14 NASB). As you can see from this verse, the apostle Paul's prayer was that we would live in active, continual fellowship with the Holy Spirit. The second way that I fellowship with the Spirit is by talking

to Him. We must understand that the Holy Spirit is a Person. He is God, and we must deliberately and actively engage Him through talking to Him. My friend, Mike Bickle, the director of the International House of Prayer (IHOP), says this: *"You will walk in the Spirit to the degree that you talk to the Spirit."*

I like to do this many times throughout my day. I love to engage the Holy Spirit and talk to Him as a Person. When I do this, I first visualize the Person of the Holy Spirit living inside of me. There is a principle in the Word of God that I call the Beholding and Becoming Principle: what we behold is what we become. In Second Corinthians 3:18, Paul says,

> *But we all, with unveiled face, beholding as in a mirror the glory of the Lord, are being transformed into the same image from glory to glory, just as by the Spirit of the Lord.*

It is as we behold with our mind's eye the glory of the Lord living on the inside of us that we are transformed day by day into His image.

Many believers struggle with this principle because the transformation does not happen instantaneously. In First Corinthians 13:12, Paul acknowledges that we do not see the fullness of God's glory now; we see Him as in a mirror, dimly, but we do see Him. And over time, bit by bit, His glory will transform us. What we behold is what we become. Therefore, when we behold the glory of God, we are conformed to His heart, His mind, and His life. He begins to change our thought life, renew our emotional chemistry, and sanctify us—body, soul, and spirit. Paul makes this same point in Romans 8:5 when he declares that *"those who live according to the flesh set their minds on the things of the flesh, but those who live according to the Spirit, the things of the Spirit."* In other words, if we want to walk in full agreement with the Spirit, we must set our minds on God. We can't measure this transformation on a daily basis, but if we determine to regularly behold the glory of the Holy Spirit dwelling within us, we will find ourselves thinking, feeling, and acting differently as the months and years progress. We will end up looking like the Holy Spirit.

So how do we behold the Spirit? There are several different descriptions of the Holy Spirit in the Word of God. In Acts 2:2, He is described as wind; in Exodus 3, He is described as fire; in John 7:37-39, He is described as a river; and in Second Corinthians 3:18, He is described as light and glory. In the middle of the day, I will close my eyes and picture one of these four realities deep in the core of my being.[7] As I do this, I intentionally quiet my soul. In Psalm 131:2, we see how the psalmist calmed and quieted his soul before approaching God. Many charismatics think that God is only heard in the lightning and the thunder, but in First Kings 19:12 God revealed that He often speaks in a still, small voice. We must quiet the traffic in our minds and hearts in order to dialogue with the Holy Spirit.

After calming my soul down and picturing the reality of the indwelling Spirit, I will talk to Him. Here in Kansas City, we use the simple acronym TRUST to guide our dialogue with the Holy Spirit. The first "T" stands for "Thank You." Thanking the Holy Spirit is the simplest way to recognize His presence within us. Most believers do not take the time to acknowledge and value the presence of God within them and then wonder why they are disconnected from the reality of the indwelling Spirit. It is important to acknowledge the free gift that we were given at salvation and to thank the Holy Spirit for His presence in us. "Thank You, Holy Spirit, that You have made me Your home. I was dead, but now I am alive. Thank You that I did nothing to deserve this; it is the free gift of God. I am the temple of the living God. Thank You, Holy Spirit."

The "R" stands for "Reign in me." Romans 8:14 says, *"For as many as are led by the Spirit of God, these are sons of God."* In other words, those who are under the government of the Holy Spirit are sons of God. Most of us are led by our thoughts, emotions, and desires rather than our spirits. In order to be led by the Holy Spirit, we must submit our souls to His governance. As we pray this prayer over time, the fire of God that dwells in our spirits will begin to break out of our inner selves and transform our thought lives—the Bible calls this the renewing of the mind (see Rom. 12:2; Col. 3:10)—change our appetites, change our emotional chemistry, and even transform our will. We will begin to love what Jesus loves and hate what Jesus hates. We will walk under the government and leadership of the Spirit.

The "U" stands for "Use me." When I pray this, I ask for the release of the nine gifts of the Holy Spirit in my life (see 1 Cor. 12:8-10). I ask for open doors and divine appointments; I ask that my words and my prayers would bring life to others. "Holy Spirit, use my eyes and my words, my hands and my feet. Anoint me to do Your work."

The "S" stands for "Strengthen me." I like to pray two powerful New Testament prayers asking for strength. In Ephesians 3:16-17a, Paul prays,

> *That He would grant you, according to the riches of His glory, to be strengthened with might through His Spirit in the inner man, that Christ may dwell in your hearts through faith.*

In Colossians 1:10b-11, Paul prays that we would increase in the knowledge of God and be *"strengthened with all might, according to His glorious power, for all patience and longsuffering with joy."*

Finally, the last "T" stands for "Teach me." The greatest teacher in the world is the Holy Spirit. In First John 2:20, John writes that we have an anointing that teaches us all things. Paul, in First Corinthians 2:13, says that we speak, not in words that human wisdom teaches, but that the Holy Spirit teaches. I love to listen to sermons and read commentaries, but I have a greater resource available; I have the Holy Spirit. When I am in the middle of my day and in need of wisdom, I will ask the Holy Spirit to come and teach me. I will ask for the seven manifestations of the Spirit of God, described in Isaiah 11:2, to fill me and anoint me with wisdom.

As you pray through this acronym and develop the habit of talking with the Holy Spirit, you will begin to find that you recognize His presence and ministry more often in your life. I want to encourage you, as you pray these prayers, to take your time. Just talk to Him and go where He goes. If you only make it through the first "T"—praise God! The point is not finishing; the point is connecting.

Meditating in the Word and dialoguing with the Spirit have dramatically changed my life. I have pursued these disciplines in a deliberate way for the last 15 years, and I have seen amazing fruit in my life and ministry. However, I want to now spend the remainder of the book exploring the glory and power of speaking in tongues. *I believe that speaking in tongues is not only a powerful way to fellowship with the Spirit, but is also a key that will unlock the door to the fullness of the Spirit for the end-time Church.* If we are faithful to steward the gift of tongues and press into God through praying in the Spirit, then God will pour out greater measures of His Spirit. This principle is illustrated many times in the teachings of Jesus. If we are faithful with the little that we are given, then we will be entrusted with more (see Luke 19:11-26). I am convinced that if we pursue and cultivate the gift of tongues, it will unlock the life of God inside of us and shift us into the purposes of the Kingdom.

ENDNOTES

1. Kenneth Hagin, *I Believe in Visions* (Old Tappan, NJ: Fleming H. Revell Company, 1972), 116-117.

2. Watchman Nee, *The Spiritual Man, Vol. I* (Anaheim, CA: Living Stream Ministry, 1992), 8.

3. A.W. Tozer' *Man: The Dwelling Place of God*, compiled by Anita M. Bailey (Harrisburg, PA: Christian Publications, 1966), 3.

4. Leonard Ravenhill, "The Judgment Seat of Christ: The Judgment of Believers," www.ravenhill.org/judgment.htm (accessed August 9, 2011).

5. Hans Urs von Balthasar, *Prayer* (San Francisco, CA: Ignatius Press, 1986), 14-15.

6. For additional material on the subject of meditation, see the fifth chapter in Corey Russell's *Pursuit of the Holy* (Kansas City, MO: Forerunner Books, 2006).

7. This is not just symbolism. We have the reality of the age to come dwelling inside of us now. We can actually drink from the river that proceeds from the throne of God (see Rev. 22:1). We can experience the fire of the Spirit that burns as seven lamps before the throne in Heaven (see Rev. 4:5).

Chapter 3

"I Speak With Tongues More Than You All"

"I thank my God I speak with tongues more than you all" (1 Corinthians 14:18).

What a bold statement for Paul to make! Every time I read this verse, I picture Paul showing up at church on Sunday, looking around the room, and then boldly stating, "I prayed in tongues more than all of you this week." I then picture a guy in the back raising his hand and saying, "Paul, I had a good week." But Paul tells him to sit down, because he knows he prayed in tongues more than that guy. Though this is likely not what happened, the claim that Paul makes in this verse is so direct that we have to stop and really consider its implications. I believe that through this verse we are given an amazing insight into the apostle Paul's devotional life.

Mike Bickle once stated that it was this verse in First Corinthians that he could not ignore in his youth when he was unsure whether the gift of tongues was a gift for the Body of Christ today. Mike came from a conservative religious background. As a young man, he went to a meeting at a charismatic church and began speaking in tongues during an altar call. He went back to his leaders and described what had happened; he was very excited and wanted to bring as many people as he could to these meetings. However, his leaders told him that what he had experienced was not biblical. Mike was shocked, but because of the great respect he had for his leaders, he believed them and decided that speaking in tongues must be the greatest deception and the greatest heresy in the Body of Christ.

And so he made it his aim to talk everybody out of believing in and desiring the gift of tongues. He would actually visit college campuses and debate people publicly over this issue. But when he lay in bed at night, he kept thinking of Paul's statement in First Corinthians 14:18—*"I thank my God I speak with tongues more than you all."* This verse drove Mike crazy. As he meditated on Paul's statement, he was struck with how busy Paul must have been as a missionary, yet he found the time to pray in tongues for hours!

Although he continued to preach against this gift, Mike couldn't get away from what he had experienced, and he wanted to know the truth for himself. Finally, after several years of internally wrestling with this issue, he decided he would try praying in the Spirit every day for six months and then evaluate the fruit. By the end of the six months, he was utterly convinced that praying in the Spirit was a gift given to believers by God to strengthen them and connect them to His heart.

Take a moment and wrestle with this question yourself: How could the busiest, most effective, most anointed, and humblest person in the New Testament—the person who did more to further the Gospel than anyone in his generation—place such emphasis on praying in tongues? Today, most believers would call Paul the greatest Christian who ever lived. I had a friend recently ask me this question: "What do you think Paul's private and devotional life looked like?" We don't have many glimpses into his personal life in the New Testament, but here we are given a clear and powerful statement regarding Paul's relationship with God and his prayer life.

The Testimony of Paul

In First Corinthians 12–14, Paul was addressing a group of sincere yet immature believers. The Corinthians were zealous for the gifts of the Spirit, but their immaturity created confusion in corporate settings. In the Corinthian church, believers would simply shout in tongues without providing any interpretation; the result was a lot of chaos and very little edification.

Many believers today look at these chapters and conclude that Paul preferred prophecy over the gift of tongues: "Prophecy is better than tongues, so why bother with tongues at all?" But in context, this is not what Paul says. When tongues are not interpreted, then prophecy is better in a corporate setting because believers understand what is said and are edified, and unbelievers are not freaked out! However, Paul did not denounce the gift of tongues. He affirmed the glory of praying in the spirit while establishing guidelines to create a culture of honor—a culture that made room for the gifts of the Spirit while serving and respecting the Body. Paul's message to Corinth can be summarized thus: pray in tongues as much as possible, but *not* in a manner that will disrupt the corporate meeting.

Let's look at this verse again: *"I thank my God I speak with tongues more than you all"* (1 Cor. 14:18). This is a bold and significant statement. It reveals how heavily Paul relied on praying in tongues to build up and edify his spirit and connect with God. In his epistle to the church in Thessalonica, Paul commands the believers to *"pray without ceasing"* (1 Thess. 5:17). Paul was a man who lived in unceasing prayer, and in this verse, we have a glimpse of what that looked like. Whether he was traveling, working, discipling, or in prison, he constantly prayed in tongues. We cannot overlook this: *the mightiest apostle in Christian history declared that he prayed in tongues all the time.* What did he understand about the power of praying in the spirit?

THE WISDOM OF GOD

Paul is the greatest example of a man who understood the wisdom of God. As a Pharisee, he had the equivalent of two decades of collegiate training in religious and pharisaical studies. When it came to education and wisdom, he was the cream of the crop. It wasn't until he encountered Jesus on the road to Damascus, however, that his eyes were opened to true wisdom. In his epistle to the Philippians, Paul stated that he counted all things—including his former education, wisdom, and prestige— as loss in comparison to the excellence of knowing and understanding Christ. His encounter caused him to realize that the doorway into the Kingdom lay in childlike humility.[1]

This is the nature of our God—the God who, in His infinite wisdom, inaugurated the gift of tongues on Pentecost. On the morning of that feast day, a group of young fishermen (most still only teenagers) stumbled out of the upper room, looking drunk and babbling in other languages. Think about this: if you were God and you could use anything as the vehicle to release your will, desires, and purposes into the world, how would you have birthed the Church on the day of Pentecost? Really, how would you have done it? Where would you have placed your greatest resources of strength, wisdom, power, and wealth? And what spiritual gift would you have released to mark the beginning of the apostolic era? The truth is that most of us would probably not have made the choice that God did. He birthed His Church in tongues.

The gift of tongues does not make sense to the natural mind. I imagine that there are other, less offensive gifts God could have designed to communicate with us. Why did He choose such a messy, controversial gift to birth His Church and then institute that gift in the daily life of the believer? He knew this gift would be one of the most hotly debated topics in the Church. Why tongues? The journey to understanding tongues is, even more so, the journey to understanding God. In this book, my desire is not only to set before you the glory, power, and intimacy available to you through fellowshipping with the Holy Spirit and speaking in tongues, but also to provoke you to wrestle with whether or not you truly know God.

The truth is that we will not live a life of praying in the Spirit unless we understand the nature of the wisdom of God. Many times in the Gospels, Jesus makes it clear that unless we are converted and become like little children, we will by no means enter the Kingdom of Heaven (see Matt. 18:3). The Church in the West is in desperate need of transformation today; we must renew our minds when it comes to knowing and understanding the ways of our God.

> *"For My thoughts are not your thoughts, nor are your ways My ways," says the Lord. "For as the heavens are higher than the earth, so are My ways higher than your ways, and My thoughts than your thoughts"* (Isaiah 55:8-9).

Today we are in the midst of a war, a war between the wisdom of people and the wisdom of God. Human wisdom rests in might, riches, and significance. God's wisdom is found in seeming weakness, foolishness, and insignificance, yet His ways are eternal. In First Corinthians, Paul states that God has chosen the things that people would never choose to accomplish His will in the Earth (see 1 Cor. 1–2). You see, God is not passively enduring the ways and wisdom of this world; He is in violent opposition to the wisdom of this world. God has a controversy with the wisdom of people, and He is zealously exposing that wisdom as a useless and bankrupt way to access the Kingdom of Heaven. *"I will destroy the wisdom of the wise, and bring to nothing the understanding of the prudent"* (1 Cor. 1:19).

We must understand that only one way provides access to the Kingdom: humility. In Jesus' first recorded sermon, He declared that the poor, the hungry, and the persecuted receive His Kingdom (see Matt. 5:1-5). In fact, He went further than that: He said that the poor, the mournful, and the hungry are the happiest people in the world. Happiness is not comfort and contentment, but rather a state of disillusionment over the lack of God in our lives—this is what Jesus proclaimed in His first public message (see Matt. 5–7).

Throughout Jesus' earthly ministry, He constantly used the lowly and foolish things of the world to illustrate the entrance into the Kingdom of Heaven. From the Sermon on the Mount to His parables and healings, Jesus showed us that the Kingdom is accessible to the humble and the hungry. Twice during His ministry Jesus declared,

> *I thank You, Father, Lord of heaven and earth, that You have hidden these things from the wise and prudent and have revealed them to babes. Even so,*

Father, for so it seemed good in Your sight (Matthew 11:25-26; Luke 10:21).

This gives us incredible revelation into the nature of our God. He is the God who deliberately sets up stumbling blocks so that only the simple, the hungry, and the sincere find Him. It is often said that God offends the mind to reveal the heart. We must understand that this is what He is really like! He is the God who, when He sends His only Son to Earth, sends Him in a way that causes everyone to stumble. No one expected the glory of God to show up in a dirty Bethlehem stable, yet God chose to manifest Himself in the most offensive setting. Proverbs 25:2 declares that it is actually the glory of God to conceal a matter.

The religious leaders in Jerusalem were wise men who had studied the Scriptures and poured over the messianic prophecies, yet when God showed up in the weak form of a man from Nazareth, it deeply offended their religious wisdom and knowledge, and they stumbled over that stumbling block. In Romans, Paul writes concerning these leaders:

> *But Israel, pursuing the law of righteousness, has not attained to the law of righteousness. Why? Because they did not seek it by faith, but as it were, by the works of the law. For they stumbled at that stumbling stone. As it is written: "Behold, I lay in Zion a stumbling stone and rock of offense, and whoever believes on Him will not be put to shame"* (Romans 9:31-33).

So great was their confidence in their own wisdom that they crucified this man who claimed to be the Son of God, failing to realize that when Jesus hung bleeding on a cross between two thieves, God's wisdom and power were on full display. The silent and agonizing death of that one man disarmed principalities and broke the power of hell and the grave.

But God has chosen the foolish things of the world to put to shame the wise, and God has chosen the weak things of the world to put to shame the things which are mighty; and the base things of the world and the things which are despised God has chosen, and the things which are not, to bring to nothing the things that are, that no flesh should glory in His presence (1 Corinthians 1:27-29).

"But God has chosen"—in other words, He had a lot of options. We see in these verses that God is scanning the Earth, looking for those things that are foolish, weak, insignificant, and despised in the eyes of humanity so that He can use those things to put to shame the things that are wise, mighty, and great. It is in weakness that God's strength is made perfect (see 2 Cor. 12:9).

Paul is actually quoting Jeremiah in this passage:

Let not the wise man glory in his wisdom, let not the mighty man glory in his might, nor let the rich man glory in his riches; but let him who glories glory in this, that he understands and knows Me, that I am the Lord... (Jeremiah 9:23-24).

This theme is repeated countless times throughout the Bible. Again and again, God challenges us concerning where we choose to place our confidence, our faith, and our trust. God weighs and tests our hearts over this issue. And Paul lets us know that the reason for this is that God does not want people strutting around in their flesh, thinking they have it all. The glory of humanity, according to Jeremiah, is to understand that we are created and that God is uncreated. The people who understand this find both exaltation and demise. They come to the end of themselves, and at the end of themselves, they discover the God who will not share His glory with another—and the God who reveals His glory to the humble.

A PERSONAL, DEVOTIONAL PRAYER LANGUAGE

The subject of speaking in tongues has been controversial throughout Church history. Could it be that the gift that has stirred some of the greatest debate and division within the Body of Christ is actually the greatest key to unlocking the power of God in the Church in these last days? Could it be that the devil has worked overtime to make this a point of contention because he understands the power it will release? The enemy doesn't spend his energy on things that don't matter, but on the realities that can potentially destroy his kingdom. This is why, I believe, the subject of our prayer language has so much warfare around it.

Let me take a moment to put a few disclaimers out there. When talking about the ministry of the Holy Spirit, I like to think of Him, with us, in us, and upon us. He is with us prior to and after salvation, He is in us at salvation, and He comes upon us at the immersion into the Holy Spirit. The question of whether or not a believer speaks in tongues is not a question of salvation. Praying in the Spirit is not evidence of salvation. The day you said yes to Jesus, you received the Holy Spirit completely on that day, and by the power of your confession of Jesus Christ as your Lord, you are saved. The purpose of our immersion or baptism in the Holy Spirit is for the purpose of power in ministry, and I believe there are several of these encounters that release greater authority in our lives over a span of one's life.

I also believe that there are a number of manifestations included in the baptism of the Spirit. For some, the baptism of the Spirit releases a greater power to resist sin. Many experience overwhelming joy as their emotions are touched with the life of God and begin to align with His truth. For some, it is a dramatic experience where they seem to lose control of their bodies; for others, it is a quiet and peaceful moment of communion marked only by a few tears.[2] However, looking at the Book of Acts, we see that speaking in tongues is prominently featured as a sign of this baptism.

Looking at the stories of the early Church, it is clear that God intended for us to receive salvation, and to keep receiving fresh encounters with the Holy Spirit that strengthen and empower us in our walk. Often these fresh encounters with the Spirit manifest in the release of our prayer language. Jesus Himself taught His disciples that He would not leave them alone, but would place His Spirit in them (see John 14:16-17). Then in John 20, we see a picture of the fulfillment of this promise:

> So Jesus said to them again, "Peace to you! As the Father has sent Me, I also send you." And when He had said this, He breathed on them, and said to them, "Receive the Holy Spirit" (John 20:21-22).

Right after the resurrection, Jesus breathed on the disciples and they received the life of God within them. They were born of God and received the Holy Spirit, just as we receive His life and Spirit at the moment of salvation.

It seemed that this encounter with the resurrected Lord would not be enough for them as it related to effectively ministering this new faith. They needed the power of the Spirit resting on them. Jesus was zealous for more than His localized ministry on Earth. He wanted to go global, and He knew this wouldn't happen through His preaching ministry. It would happen when Jesus was actually in His people, resting on them in power and moving through them by the Holy Spirit. Even before His ministry began, John the Baptist identified the Christ as the One who would baptize with the Holy Spirit and fire (see Matt. 3:11; John 1:33). John knew Jesus as the baptizer.

Jesus said in Luke 12, *"I came to send fire on the earth, and how I wish it were already kindled"* (Luke 12:49). He was zealous to pour out the Spirit! The night before His crucifixion, He took great pains to talk about the Holy Spirit. Then, after He came out of the grave, He commanded the disciples to wait for the baptism of the Spirit (see Luke 24:49). Think about that for a moment. The Holy Spirit was already in them, they had already experienced the glory of the new birth, and the resurrected Christ had just spent 40 days with them, teaching them about the Kingdom, yet that wasn't enough for the Church to be birthed. They were told to wait because there was more; there was another experience of the Spirit.

> *But you shall receive power when the Holy Spirit has come upon you; and you shall be witnesses to Me in Jerusalem, and in all Judea and Samaria, and to the end of the earth* (Acts 1:8).

In Acts 2, the very disciples who had received the Spirit when Jesus breathed on them were gathered in the Upper Room, waiting as they had been told. When the day of Pentecost had fully come, there was a sound of a mighty, rushing wind, tongues of fire appeared over their heads, and they were filled with the Holy Spirit, beginning to speak with other tongues. This experience was not about the indwelling life of the Spirit; it was about power. When the Holy Spirit fell upon the disciples that day, the sheepish Peter, who had denied Jesus only weeks ago, came out of that Upper Room boldly proclaiming the Gospel, and 3,000 people were saved.

In Acts 4, two years after that day of Pentecost, the early Church encountered persecution for the first time. What was their response? The same disciples who had received the baptism of the Spirit in that Upper Room met together to pray, and when they prayed, the place where they were assembled was shaken, and they were all filled with the Holy Spirit, and then they spoke the Word of God with boldness. They received another baptism of the Spirit.

In Acts 8, we see perhaps the strongest evidence for the baptism of the Spirit after salvation. The apostles heard that the Samaritans had believed in Christ and experienced salvation (see Acts 8:4-8). In response, Peter and John travelled to Samaria to pray for these new believers to receive the Holy Spirit. They knew that there was a baptism available to the Samaritans, although the Holy Spirit had already sealed them at the moment of salvation.

> *Now when the apostles who were at Jerusalem heard that Samaria had received the word of God, they sent Peter and John to them, who, when they had come down, prayed for them that they might receive the Holy Spirit. For as yet He had fallen upon none of them. They had only been baptized in the name of the Lord Jesus. Then they laid hands on them, and they received the Holy Spirit* (Acts 8:14-17).

Similarly, in Acts 19, Paul visited Ephesus and asked if they had received the Holy Spirit when they believed.

> *...So they said to him, "We have not so much as heard whether there is a Holy Spirit." And he said to them, "Into what then were you baptized?" So they said, "Into John's baptism." Then Paul said, "John indeed baptized with a baptism of repentance, saying to the people that they should believe on Him who would come after him, that is, on Christ Jesus." When they heard this, they were baptized in the name of the Lord Jesus. And when Paul had laid hands on them, the Holy Spirit came upon*

them, and they spoke with tongues and prophesied (Acts
19:2-6).

It is clear from these verses that the people heard the Gospel
and accepted Jesus, and at that moment of salvation, they were
sealed with the indwelling Holy Spirit (see Eph. 1:13). But then
Paul laid hands on them, and the Holy Spirit came upon them,
and they spoke with tongues and prophesied. These stories of the
early Church found in the Book of Acts demonstrate again and
again that believers receive the Spirit at more than just an initial
conversion, but they receive frequent outpourings, or "baptisms,"
that release, among other things, the gift of tongues.

Now let me take a moment to clarify what I mean when I
speak of the gift of tongues. There are a few expressions of this
gift highlighted in the New Testament.[3] In First Corinthians 12,
Paul clearly seems to be referring to a gift of tongues that functions in a corporate setting:

> *Are all apostles? Are all prophets? Are all teachers? Are*
> *all workers of miracles? Do all have gifts of healings?*
> *Do all speak with tongues? Do all interpret?* (1 Corin-
> thians 12:29-30)

This passage suggests that there are individuals with a specific gift of tongues who, when they operate in this gift *and*
provide interpretation, edify and strengthen the corporate body in
a similar fashion to someone with the gift of prophecy, teaching,
or healing. But this is not the expression of tongues I am highlighting in this book.

In Acts 2, when the disciples began to speak in other tongues,
the Jews from the Diaspora who had gathered in Jerusalem for
the Feast of Pentecost each heard the Gospel proclaimed in their
own language (see Acts 2:5-11). This is another expression of the
gift of tongues—the miraculous ability to speak a language one
hasn't learned. This gift of tongues is most often released for the

purposes of evangelism. I have a friend from Mozambique who has operated in this gift on many occasions. He has traveled to various remote tribes in Africa, stood up to preach without any knowledge of their specific dialect, and miraculously received the ability to speak that dialect as he began to preach. This is definitely an expression of the gift of tongues that I value and desire, but it is not the focus of this book.

What I want to talk about for the next several chapters is the glorious reality of our personal prayer language—the gift of tongues that is available to all believers for their own devotional lives. In First Corinthians 14:27-28, Paul gives directions to individuals who wish to speak in tongues:

> *If anyone speaks in a tongue, let there be two or at the*
> *most three, each in turn, and let one interpret. But if*
> *there is no interpreter, let him keep silent in church,*
> *and let him speak to himself and to God.*

In these directions, Paul assumes that there is an experience of the life and power of the Holy Spirit available to all believers: the personal, devotional gift of tongues. He taught the Corinthians that when we speak in tongues, it is a private conversation between our spirits and the Spirit of God. Paul considered this expression of tongues so important that, earlier in the chapter, he declared that he wished all believers spoke in tongues (see 1 Cor. 14:5a).

I believe that God is bringing a generation back to this gift that fueled the man whose conversion and apostolic ministry is one of the strongest testimonies of the resurrection of Jesus. Paul's testimony is not the only apostolic testimony when it comes to the power of tongues. The same witness exists in recent history. John G. Lake, a missionary and revivalist who moved in powerful signs and wonders, declared that "tongues has been the making of my ministry."[4] It is said that Smith Wigglesworth, a great leader of the Pentecostal revival in the late 19th century who was noted for his healing ministry, spent at least an hour every morning praying in tongues.[5]

We are hearing a lot in recent years about the restoration of the apostolic ministry, and I am convinced that at the forefront of this restoration there will be an exponential increase in praying in the Spirit. I desire to see this reality sweep across the Body of Christ, transcending denomination and affiliation.

ENDNOTES

1. I do not mean to dismiss the value or necessity of deep theological training and study. These things are valuable, but they must not be the foundation of our confidence.

2. Shelley Hundley, "Transformation and the Four Forms of Prayer," lecture (Kansas City, MO: IHOPU, February 10, 2011).

3. It is common for scholars to recognize two forms of speaking in tongues or *glossolalia* (the Greek term used in the New Testament): Spirit-inspired speech that is unknown to both speaker and hearer (Paul's "tongues of angels" in 1 Corinthians 13:1) and Spirit-inspired speech that is unknown to the speaker but known to the hearer (Paul's "tongues of men" in 1 Corinthians 13:1, which refers to actual human language). For a more in-depth study of this subject, I highly recommend Christopher Forbes' *Prophecy and Inspired Speech in Early Christianity and its Hellenistic Environment*. I agree with this standard dualistic definition of the gift of tongues and would only add that I believe the personal, devotional use of tongues is a private expression of the gift of heavenly or angelic language.

4. John G. Lake, "The Baptism of the Holy Ghost," in *John G. Lake: His Life, His Sermons, His Boldness of Faith* (Fort Worth, TX: Kenneth Copeland Publications, 1994), 485.

5. This quote about Smith Wigglesworth is just a known fact. I don't have a concrete reference for that quote.

Chapter 4

Unlocking Mysteries

Once during a prayer meeting, a friend of mine was praying in the spirit on the microphone. That day a Native American chief happened to be visiting the prayer room. After the meeting, he approached a leader and asked about the woman praying on the microphone. He said she was speaking in his native tongue when she prayed, although it was a dialect no longer spoken. When asked to translate what she was saying, the chief shared that she had prayed again and again, "Jesus, hold me like a mother holds her child."

I love this story because it reveals the deep intimacy that was flowing from the Holy Spirit through my friend as she prayed in the Spirit. This story illustrates the fundamental purpose of our prayer language. Romans 8:15 says that we have received the spirit of adoption by which we cry out *"Abba, Father!"* When we pray in tongues, the Holy Spirit within us releases deep and intimate truths that ascend straight to the throne of God. The chief heard my friend praying, "Jesus, hold me like a mother holds her child"—how tender and profound. These are the prayers and truths that flow out of our spirits when we speak in tongues. Paul calls these truths "mysteries." In his letter to the Corinthians, he states that we speak these mysteries straight to God when we pray in the Spirit. This letter provides us with some of the greatest insight into the unique dynamics of speaking in tongues found in the New Testament.

SPEAKING STRAIGHT TO GOD

For he who speaks in a tongue does not speak to men but to God, for no one understands him; however, in the spirit he speaks mysteries (1 Corinthians 14:2).

When I speak and teach on the glory and benefit of tongues, I like to begin with this verse. Here, Paul makes two incredibly significant statements about speaking in tongues. First, he declares that when we speak in tongues we speak to God and God alone. Then he says that when we speak in tongues, we are actually speaking mysteries. I want to spend some time examining both of these statements closely, for they each hold great depths of treasure and revelation. In fact, these statements address two of the greatest hindrances we will face as we begin to engage in praying in the Spirit on a consistent basis. The first hindrance is this: when we pray in the Spirit it is easy to feel disconnected from the reality of the conversation because we do not know to whom we are speaking. Fortunately, Paul addresses this in his letter to the church at Corinth. He reminds the Corinthians that when they speak in tongues, they are speaking directly to God. They are not filling the air with sound, and they are not emptying their minds by speaking gibberish. *They are talking to God.*

When we pray in the Spirit, we are not engaging people or angels or demons or anything else; we are connecting with our Father in a personal, private conversation. When Jesus taught the disciples how to pray, He began by telling them to address a

Person: *"Our Father in heaven, hallowed be Your name..."* (Luke 11:2). Then He poured out His Spirit so that all of His disciples might *experience* constant communion with God. Remember the umbilical cord analogy? We are directly connected with God by the Holy Spirit. And this is not a one-way connection. We have been given the Spirit for the purpose of dialogue and communion with God. The Holy Spirit dwelling within us longs to release language that produces communion. In Song of Solomon, the Lord expresses His desire for communion: *"...Let me see your face, let me hear your voice; for your voice is sweet, and your face is lovely"* (Song of Sol. 2:14b). He not only wants to be united with us by the Spirit, He wants us to talk directly to Him in the Spirit. He wants to hear our voice.

Stop for a moment and consider the glory of this truth. Not many people have access to the President of the United States; average civilians will probably never sit in the Oval Office and talk with the leader of the free world. But we have a direct phone line to the Creator of the universe. He longs for us to speak straight to Him, regardless of our circumstances. God has invited us into His inner circle—into the conversation of the Trinity—and given us everything we need to commune with Him, spirit-to-Spirit.

It is important to remember that prayer is a dialogue; we should expect God to respond when we speak to Him. Sometimes He will respond by speaking with a still, small voice in our spirits or moving in our hearts with gentle thoughts and impressions; other times, He will respond by renewing our minds, transforming our thought lives and emotional chemistry, and refreshing our spirits. Regardless of whether or not we hear a thunderous voice from Heaven, when we speak to God in tongues, we can know with confidence that He is answering. The Creator of the universe is talking back to us.

I have been consistently praying in the Spirit for over a decade now, and I have found that rooting my mind in the reality that I am speaking directly to God releases the grace that I need to continue the conversation. And one of the most effective ways that I have found to do this is through fixing my mind's eye on the Person with whom I am speaking. For many, the most important key to persevering in praying in the Spirit is creating a focal point for the mind's eye. This is so important because many believers, when they go to speak in tongues, just shoot their words into the air: they talk to the air, as if no one was listening; then they get disconnected, they lose heart, and eventually they stop praying in the Spirit at all. The power of praying in tongues is that we are talking to a Person. It is often when we find a focal point that we experience grace and longevity.

When I speak in tongues, there are two focal points that I use, both of which are found in the Scriptures: God on the throne and God in my spirit. I like to call it God eternal and God internal. When I focus on the eternal God on the throne, I love to picture the scene from Revelation 4. The apostle John is caught up in the spirit, and he sees a throne seated above every throne.

The One sitting on that throne is shining like a diamond, burning like fire, and surrounded by an emerald rainbow. This is our Father: He's the most beautiful Person we've ever met, the most passionate Person we've ever met, and the most compassionate Person we've ever met—full of covenantal mercy. Lightnings, thunderings, and voices emanate from this throne, and seven lamps of fire are burning before it—the seven spirits of God. Before the throne of God there's a sea of glass like crystal, a sea of glass mingled with flaming fire.

Every time I pray in tongues, I stand on that sea of glass, I lift my hands, and I gaze upon the One on the throne. And I am not the only one gazing; there are those creatures with eyes around and within. They're called seraphim—the burning ones. They do not rest day or night, saying, "Holy, holy, holy, Lord God Almighty." Beloved, we were made to burn like the seraphim. We were made to gaze on God. And when we behold His glory, we're transformed into the same image. That is God eternal.

But God is not only eternal. God is also internal: *"Christ in you, the hope of glory"* (Col. 1:27). God is in our spirits. In the second chapter, I talked about the descriptions of the Holy Spirit found in the Scriptures: He is like wind, fire, a river, and glory. As I pray in the Spirit, I close my eyes and picture one of these realities. I picture the shekinah glory of God burning inside of me like a brilliant light, and I speak to that glory.

I want to make it clear that it is not necessary to create a focal point in order to successfully speak in tongues. You can speak in tongues without involving your imagination and still connect with God. However, I have found that rooting my mind in the Word as I pray in the Spirit has been the most effective way of connecting with God and persevering in this gift. In Colossians 3 we are commanded to set our minds on things above (see Col. 3:1-2). These verses describe a diligent seeking of Heaven; we are called to take our thought lives and fill them with the reality of God. Filling our minds with the Word, as we pray in the Spirit, is one of the most powerful ways to do this.

It has taken a long time for God eternal and God internal to begin to become fixed realities in my mind. The first time I heard someone preach on Revelation 4 was in 1999, and I didn't know what the person was talking about. It was only after several years of regularly reading the chapter that it became a fixed reality that I experienced when I closed my eyes. We are called to love God with all of our minds, and engaging our imagination is part of loving God with our minds. We are actually sanctifying our imaginations when we use them to picture the realities described in the Bible. Most of our lives we spend inside our minds, and we can't turn them off, so we need to learn how to use our thought lives and our imagination to love God!

We know now that we are invited into a conversation, and we have been given everything we need to fix our minds' eye on the Person we are speaking to. But this conversation is not in English or Chinese or Russian or Spanish or any other human language. John 4:23 states that God is Spirit and that those who worship Him must worship in spirit and truth. God is Spirit, and He communicates in the Spirit, by the Spirit. This means that when we speak in tongues, we are addressing God in His native tongue: spirit. The gift of tongues is the reality of the Holy Spirit speaking a distinct and specific language to God through us—a language that He understands. There is much comfort and strength to be derived from the revelation that we are speaking straight to the heart of God and that He understands us, even when we don't understand ourselves. When we pray in the Spirit, we're not babbling to the air; we're communicating with a Person in a specific language.

During World War II, the United States Marines used a code created by Navajo Indians to send messages between fronts. The Axis powers were unable to break this code because the Navajo language was known by very few and was incredibly difficult to learn. The Navajo who created and translated this code were known as windtalkers. Mahesh Chavda, a powerful evangelist and revivalist in the Church today, talks about the picture of speaking in tongues these windtalkers have given us:

> This story of the Navajo windtalkers brought to my mind a connection with those believers long ago who talked into the "wind" of Pentecost. The Greek word *pneuma*, which is often translated "spirit," also means

"breath" or "wind." The 120 believers gathered in that upper room heard "a sound from heaven, as of a rushing mighty wind," and they "began to speak with other tongues." These newly Spirit-filled believers were spiritual "windtalkers." They spoke in a new language that was like a "breath" of heaven.

Just as the Japanese could not penetrate the code of the Navajo windtalkers, so the devil cannot break through the language of the Spirit. Speaking in tongues is a heavenly communication, a language that links us with the glory of God. It puts us in tune with His heart and mind. Just as the Navajo windtalkers alone could understand each other in their unique tongue, so also do spiritual windtalkers have a secure communication with the Lord, a special language or "code" that cannot be intercepted, understood or subverted by the enemy. Speaking in tongues is the language of the realm of heaven.[1]

This is the first hindrance Paul addresses. We will not successfully engage long-term in praying in the Spirit if we are not rooted and grounded in the reality that we are speaking directly to God. He then says that when we speak in tongues, we speak mysteries in the Spirit. This statement addresses a second hindrance. When we pray in the Spirit, it is easy to feel disconnected from the reality of the conversation because we do not understand what we are saying. According to Paul, however, it is possible to know the content of our conversation in the Spirit: we are speaking mysteries. In Paul's letters specifically, and in the New Testament in general, the word *mystery* refers to those things that were hidden in the heart of God throughout the Old Testament and unveiled through the ministry of Christ and the revelation of the Holy Spirit.[2]

THE MYSTERIES OF GOD

We were made to discover the deep things of God. We were designed for the glory and drama of searching out His mysteries: *"...It is the glory of God to conceal a matter, but the glory of kings is to search out a matter"* (Prov. 25:2). Why would God establish His Kingdom on the principle of hide-and-seek? The answer lies in the fact that we were created for relationship with God. We were made for communion—for relational connection with the living God—so He designed our hearts to run on fresh encounter and fresh revelation.

Proverbs 29:18 says that the absence of revelation leads to sin and death. It is only through encountering the mysteries of God's heart that our hearts are awakened and sustained and we discover true life. Not only are we sustained when we encounter God in new and deeper ways, but He is magnified when we spend our lives searching for the mysteries of His heart. God receives greater glory when He hides the deep things of His heart because it draws people after Him to search carefully and diligently for these deep things as for treasure.

> *My son, if you receive my words, and treasure my commands within you, so that you incline your ear to wisdom, and apply your heart to understanding; yes, if you cry out for discernment, and lift up your voice for understanding, if you seek her as silver, and search for her as for hidden treasures; then you will understand the fear of the Lord, and find the knowledge of God* (Proverbs 2:1-5).

This is why the mysteries of God are not unknowable; they were established in order that we might find them. Jesus told the disciples that it was given to them to know the mysteries of the

Kingdom. God desires to give the mysteries of the Kingdom to us! *Mysteries aren't things that are hidden from us, but things that are hidden for us.* They aren't things that can never be known, but things that are hidden for the purpose of being found.

I like to use the example of parents hiding Easter eggs for their children. (Don't stress out because I've mentioned Easter eggs. I do not actually hide eggs for my children and then tell them the Easter Bunny visited us, but I still think it is a good illustration.) As a father I don't try to prove my superiority by hiding the Easter eggs in impossible-to-find places. I hide them so that my kids will experience the excitement of the search and the delight of the discovery. The same is true of hide-and-seek. The point is not to hide so that my kids can't find me; the point is to be found. Our Father is no different. He wants us to experience the excitement of searching for Him and the delight of finding Him. God hides to be found.

> *Again, the kingdom of heaven is like treasure hidden in a field, which a man found and hid; and for joy over it he goes and sells all that he has and buys that field* (Matthew 13:44).

The aim and the goal of the searching is joy!

In Luke 10, the 70 disciples, who were sent out to proclaim the Kingdom of God to the surrounding towns and villages, returned to Jesus, bringing stories of healing, deliverance, and salvation. Look at Jesus' response:

> *In that hour Jesus rejoiced in the Spirit and said, "I thank You, Father, Lord of heaven and earth, that You have hidden these things from the wise and prudent and revealed them to babes. Even so, Father, for so it seemed good in Your sight"* (Luke 10:21).

It says that He rejoiced in the Spirit; in other words, He was overwhelmed with joy by the Father's ways. "Father, I love how You run Your Kingdom. You hide these things from the proud and reveal them to the hungry and the humble."

Many believers feel rejected or abandoned when they can't find God right away. They think He is a mean God who doesn't want to be found by them, or they think He is distant and uncaring— too preoccupied to notice their searching. The truth, though, is that God is drawing them out. In Song of Solomon 3, the young woman is provoked to go and search for her Beloved:

> *By night on my bed I sought the one I love; I sought him, but I did not find him. "I will rise now," I said, "and go about the city; in the streets and in the squares I will seek the one I love." I sought him, but I did not find him. The watchmen who go about the city found me; I said, "Have you seen the one I love?" Scarcely had I passed by them, when I found the one I love* (Song of Solomon 3:1-4a).

Song of Solomon gives us a picture of the relationship between Jesus and His Bride. In these verses, we see that there are times when God draws away from us so that we become desperate. Once we decide to step away from everything that is comfortable and familiar and convenient in order to search for Him, we will be surprised at how quickly we find Him!

Once we have a correct paradigm, we will begin to find life and joy in the pursuit of the mysteries of God. I like to think of these mysteries in four broad categories, each of which are enormous in scope. Although this list of categories is not comprehensive, I believe that the majority of the mysteries that we release through speaking in tongues fit into these four categories. First, when I pray in the Spirit, I am speaking mysteries about God—who He is, how He feels, and what He is like. This category represents the realm of the knowledge of God. Second, when I pray in the Spirit, I am speaking mysteries about myself—who I am in Him and my divine destiny. When I speak in tongues, I actually prophesy my divine destiny. Third, when I pray in the Spirit I am speaking mysteries about His plans—the things burning on His heart, His thoughts and purposes, the new things that He is releasing today, and the issues that He is addressing. And fourth, when I pray in the Spirit, I am speaking mysteries about people in need. This could be someone who I will meet later in the day at the grocery store, a friend I haven't spoken to recently, a loved one, or a spouse.

Many times when I am praying in the Spirit, I will find myself thinking of someone I haven't seen in years. Often, I will see or hear from that person later in the day. This used to shock me, but over time I have grown to expect it. Now if the Lord brings someone to mind while I am praying in tongues, I will begin to intercede for the person and to release blessings over him or her. Then when I run into that person later, or receive a phone call or an E-mail, I am able to bless him or her in the way that God leads me. I recognize that my spirit has been prepared to minister to that individual, and I am filled with the faith that I need for the moment. Sometimes I am led to bless him or her financially, other times to pray for him or her and release prophetic words of encouragement. Whatever the need may be, I am actually carrying a deposit in my spirit that is meant for that person, and I have gradually learned to partner with the Lord in releasing that deposit. This is one of the ways that the mysteries of God's heart are made known to His Body.

Paul was gripped with the mysteries of God. His letters to the churches are filled with revelation concerning these mysteries. In Romans, Paul writes that he does not want the believers to be ignorant of the mystery of God's plan (see Rom. 11:25). In other words, Paul believed that it was the inheritance of every Christian to know and understand the mysteries of God. He did not want a single believer to be ignorant of the deep things of God's heart. He understood these mysteries as centerpieces of revelation and information that are available to all believers. When Paul declared something to be a mystery, he was actually inviting believers into the revelation of Christ and all that was accomplished through His life, death, resurrection, and ascension. He now beckons the hungry to come through this doorway, to come and see.

There are six specific mysteries that Paul highlights in his letters—all of which are fundamentally related to the revelation of Christ. Beloved, we need the revelation of Christ Jesus and all that will be brought about through Him. I believe that when we pray in tongues we are actually probing the mind of God concerning these things. Here are the mysteries that Paul references:

> *...By revelation He made known to me the mystery (as I have briefly written already, by which, when you read, you may understand my knowledge in the mystery of Christ), which in other ages was not made known to the sons of men, as it has now been revealed by the Spirit to His holy apostles and prophets: that the Gentiles should be fellow heirs, of the same body, and partakers of His promise in Christ through the gospel* (Ephesians 3:3-6).

> *This is a great mystery* [Bride and Bridegroom], *but I speak concerning Christ and the church* (Ephesians 5:32).

> *For I do not desire brethren that you should be ignorant of this mystery* [Israel and Church], *lest you*

should be wise in your own opinion, that blindness in part has happened to Israel until the fullness of the Gentiles has come in (Romans 11:25).

Behold, I tell you a mystery [resurrection from the dead]*: We shall not all sleep, but we shall all be changed* (1 Corinthians 15:51).

To them God willed to make known what are the riches of the glory of this mystery among the Gentiles: which is Christ in you, the hope of glory (Colossians 1:27).

For the mystery of lawlessness is already at work (2 Thessalonians 2:7a).

The main component of the apostolic Gospel is the revelation of the mysteries of God. It is no coincidence that the man who spoke in tongues more than anyone is the same man who walked in the greatest revelation of the mysteries of God. Today, we are in an hour of the restoration of apostolic Christianity. As we engage with these mysteries through praying in the Spirit, we are going to see these realities connected to Christ and the Gospel released on the Earth in a greater way. We are in the midst of a transformation in the Body of Christ, and this transformation is about bringing the Church back to its apostolic foundations. What was the early Church, as well as today's Church, built on? It was built on the revelation of Jesus Christ.

As we speak in tongues, we are declaring these very mysteries: *"He who speaks in a tongue…in the spirit he speaks mysteries"* (1 Cor. 14:2). We are speaking heavenly things that our minds do not yet understand, but as we pray in the Spirit, God releases these mysteries through our mouths and into our spirits so we may receive the deep things of His heart.

..."Eye has not seen, nor ear heard, nor have entered into the heart of man the things which God has prepared for those who love Him." But God has revealed them to us through His Spirit (1 Corinthians 2:9-10a).

The mysteries of the Kingdom—the things that God has prepared for us—are meant to be unlocked as we speak in tongues.

THE SPIRIT OF REVELATION

The apostle Paul was a man of revelation. He was given so much revelation that there was a perpetual attack from the enemy to keep him humble (see 2 Cor. 12:7). There are several factors that play in the abundance of revelation that operated in him and his ministry, but none as intriguing as praying in the Spirit. He understood that to grow in the revelation of Christ, he must constantly engage the revelation of the Holy Spirit through speaking in tongues and declaring mysteries in the Spirit. When we pray in tongues, we pray into the realm of the Spirit—the place of revelation where divine mysteries are unlocked and communicated to our spirits. It is true that, as believers, we have the Holy Spirit, but we need to get into the realm of the Spirit.

I like to use the analogy of radio signals: most of us live our lives tuned into AM, but God is on FM. We have to change the signal we are receiving; we have to get into the Spirit to hear from God. The greatest and most precious commodity in the life of a believer today is the Spirit of revelation. In Ephesians 1:16-19, Paul prayed for the church of Ephesus that the Father of glory would give to them the Spirit of revelation and that their spiritual senses would be awakened to see, hear, perceive, and know the deep things of God.

*Therefore I also, after I heard of your faith in the
Lord Jesus and your love for all the saints, do not cease
to give thanks for you, making mention of you in my
prayers: that the God of our Lord Jesus Christ, the
Father of glory, may give to you the spirit of wisdom
and revelation in the knowledge of Him, the eyes of
your understanding being enlightened; that you may
know what is the hope of His calling, what are the
riches of the glory of His inheritance in the saints, and
what is the exceeding greatness of His power toward us
who believe* (Ephesians 1:15-19a).

*For the Spirit searches all things, yes, the deep things
of God. For what man knows the things of a man
except the spirit of the man which is in him? Even
so no one knows the things of God except the Spirit
of God. Now we have received, not the spirit of the
world, but the Spirit who is from God, that we might
know the things that have been freely given to us by
God* (1 Corinthians 2:10b-12).

According to First Corinthians, one of the Holy Spirit's main
job descriptions is to search out the deep things of God (His mysteries) and make them known to the redeemed. As we engage the
Holy Spirit through praying in the Spirit, we are actually being
filled with the things that are burning on His heart. We have
been given the Holy Spirit so that God might take us on a guided
tour of Himself. The Holy Spirit is the search engine—the Spirit
that searches all things, even the deep things of God—and we
have received Him so that we might know the things that have
been freely given us by God.

Romans 8:26 states, *"For we do not know what we should pray
for as we ought, but the spirit Himself makes intercession for us with*

groanings which cannot be uttered." As we pray in tongues, the Holy Spirit, the One who searches the deep things of God, is releasing out of our mouths the perfect will of the Father into existence. He is praying through us, for us, and with us to bring forth the plans and purposes of the Father. These are the mysteries that we were made by God to receive and release.

> *All things have been delivered to Me by My Father, and no one knows the Son except the Father. Nor does anyone know the Father except the Son, and the one to whom the Son wills to reveal Him* (Matthew 11:27; see Luke 10:22).

Jesus declared that the way to know the Father was through revelation. I often pray, "Let me be the one to whom the Son reveals the Father." While He lived on Earth, Jesus revealed the heart of the Father through His own life. After His death and ascension, He poured out His Spirit so that He might continue to reveal God to us. This is why we have been given the Spirit: so that we might know God and our inheritance in Him through the revelation of the Holy Spirit.

The Holy Spirit Is the Revealer of Truth

> *I still have many things to say to you, but you cannot bear them now. However, when He, the Spirit of truth, has come, He will guide you into all truth; for He will not speak on His own authority, but whatever He hears He will speak; and He will tell you things to come. He will glorify Me, for He will take of what is Mine and declare it to you. All things that the Father has are Mine. Therefore I said that He will take of Mine and declare it to you* (John 16:12-15).

As I read this passage, I can picture Jesus looking at the disciples and longing to share the deepest things of His heart with them. He wanted to blow their minds with the revelation of the glory to come, but He knew they were already overwhelmed by what He had shared. He must have rejoiced in the fact that the Holy Spirit was coming, and that His role would be to take believers on a tour into the depths of truth. In these verses Jesus states that just as a tour guide leads people into unknown territory, so the Holy Spirit, as a divine guide, will lead the hungry and the prepared into the revelation of the mystery of Christ Jesus.

The Holy Spirit Is the Revealer of the Trinity

Verses 14-15 of the same passage state that the Holy Spirit will openly declare to those who have ears to hear whatever is shared between God the Father and God the Son; He will bring us into the conversation of the Godhead. I remember when I was first struck with this passage. For months I was constantly asking, "Holy Spirit, what are You hearing?" John tells us that whatever the Holy Spirit hears as the third Person of the Trinity, He will speak. He actually wants to reveal the conversations of God to us. I want to know what He longs to tell me! I want a fresh revelation every day that awakens my faith and escorts me into the realm of the spirit. What are the Father, Son, and Spirit talking about right now?

The Holy Spirit Is the Revealer of the Future

Not only does the Holy Spirit tell us what He is hearing presently, but He also tells us things to come. He is a prophetic Spirit who desires to unfold the future. What is God saying right now about the hour of history in which we live? What is He about to unfold on the planet? We have been given access to all things in

Christ, and it is the Holy Spirit's job to communicate all things to us—including things that have not yet taken place.

The Holy Spirit Is the Revealer of the Glories of the Age to Come

Amazingly, Paul does not simply state that we will be overwhelmed one day when we finally enter into the next age. Instead, he says that the realities that will be fully manifested in the next age are available to us now through the Holy Spirit. The day that we said yes to Jesus, God placed His Spirit in us as a guarantee of the age to come. We have, living inside of us, the foretaste of eternal glories. The Spirit is God's earnest, His down payment, His guarantee that He will return and complete the work that He began at His first coming.

> In Him you also trusted, after you heard the word of truth, the gospel of your salvation; in whom also, having believed, you were sealed with the Holy Spirit of promise, who is the guarantee of our inheritance until the redemption of the purchased possession, to the praise of His glory (Ephesians 1:13-14).

> ..."Eye has not seen, nor ear heard, nor have entered into the heart of man the things which God has prepared for those who love Him." But God has revealed them to us through His Spirit (1 Corinthians 2:9-10a).

The things that God has reserved for those who love Him will be fully manifested in the age to come. However, Paul tells us that through the Holy Spirit we can experience a "sneak peek" of those things in this age. We can actually taste the powers of the age to come today. It is these tokens that produce in us a longing for the fullness that will be released at the second coming of Jesus. The Holy Spirit is the token, the down payment, the guarantee of our coming glory. Once the Holy Spirit comes to live inside of us, He produces a longing for eternity in our hearts. In Romans 8:15, Paul tells us that we have received the spirit of adoption by whom we cry out Abba Father. Eight verses later, Paul tells us that the adoption that we are crying out for is actually the redemption of our bodies. As the Holy Spirit reveals more and more of eternity to our hearts, we cry out increasingly for the work of sanctification and glorification to be completed and for the transformation of even our physical bodies (see 2 Cor. 5:1-5).

This is our portion: to know the mysteries of God. The Holy Spirit has been given to us to reveal these mysteries. And the gift of tongues has been given to us so that we might engage the Holy Spirit and release that revelation. When we speak in tongues, we are awakening our spiritual senses and engaging this Spirit of revelation. Revelation is the ground on which faith stands. Revelation opens us up to all that is available to us in Christ. It makes known that which was concealed before—the plan of redemption hidden in the heart of God. Revelation takes us into the knowledge of God. This is why the greatest need in every believer's life is the Spirit of revelation. Revelation makes known to us our inheritance, and once we see and know what we have been given and who God is, we are empowered to step out in faith. Faith flows from revelation; our ability to step out into the unseen is directly proportionate to the degree of revelation that we possess. Therefore, our greatest need is an ever-increasing Spirit of revelation.

Praying in the Spirit Is Critical to Engaging the Revelatory Realm

When we speak in tongues, we are not only proclaiming the mysteries of God, but we are also engaging the Spirit of revelation that will unlock those mysteries for us. This means that by praying in the Spirit we are actually preparing ourselves to walk in greater measures of faith. I find on a regular basis that after praying in tongues for 20 minutes my mind begins to be filled and flooded with divine thoughts, verses, and impressions. This revelation usually takes the form of verses and phrases in the Bible that are suddenly highlighted in my mind, connections between various Scriptures, words of knowledge, words of wisdom, or pictures and visions. Even my dream life changes when I am spending regular amounts of time praying in the Spirit.

As you speak in tongues, you will find the Word of God opening to your mind, you will see an increase in divine appointments, and your thoughts and emotions will begin to carry the anointing of God.

I believe that as we consistently pray in the Spirit, God will answer us with invitations to come up higher and receive greater impartations of revelation. The apostle John was on the island of Patmos when he was given a holy invitation into the realm of the Spirit to unlock divine mysteries. These mysteries became the Book of Revelation.

> *After these things I looked, and behold, a door standing open in heaven. And the first voice which I heard was like a trumpet speaking with me, saying, "Come up here, and I will show you things which must take place after this." Immediately I was in the Spirit* (Revelation 4:1-2a).

ENDNOTES

1. Mahesh Chavda, *The Hidden Power of Speaking in Tongues* (Shippensburg, PA: Destiny Image Publishers, 2003), 13.

2. James Strong, *The Strongest Strong's Exhaustive Concordance of the Bible,* 21st century ed., fully rev. by John R. Kohlenberger III and James A. Swanson (Grand Rapids, MI: Zondervan, 2001), 1516.

Chapter 5

STRENGTHENING YOURSELF

I have a good friend who spent time in Bolivia as a missionary. While she was there, she attended a small house church where the members were encouraged to pray in tongues all the time. Working, shopping, socializing—no matter what activity they were engaged in, these believers thought that they should be praying in the Spirit under their breath. The fruit of this lifestyle was dramatic. That small congregation witnessed many powerful miracles on a regular basis because of their lifestyle of fellowshipping with the Holy Spirit. One of the most dramatic stories she heard during her time there involved a tractor driver and his co-worker. This man worked on a soybean plantation and he spent most of his days praying in tongues as he drove his tractor. One day his co-worker failed to show up for his shift. At the end of the day, the man went over to the little tin shack where the man lived. He knocked on the door, and then the stench hit him; he could smell the corpse. He broke open the door and discovered that the man had hung himself the night before.

Immediately, his flesh wanted to run from the gruesome sight and smell, but his spirit drew him into the shack. He cut the man down, laid him on the ground, and began to pray in tongues. After a little while, this phrase came to him: "Jesus, I praise You because You are life." He began to declare that phrase and continued praying in the Spirit. Suddenly the corpse sat up! Again, his flesh wanted to run—after all, he was in this little shack with a moving corpse, and that is enough to freak anyone out—but his spirit compelled him to keep praying. He was so used to being led by his communion with the Holy Spirit that he continued to intercede. After a little while longer, the man was finally restored to life. He received the Gospel and the baptism of the Holy Spirit that same night and became a devoted follower of Jesus.[1]

What I love about this story is the reality that all of the tractor driver's natural tendencies were urging him to run away. His physical senses were repulsed by the sight and smell of death, and his mind told him that it was too late and nothing could be done for his former co-worker. But his spirit drew him into the shack and led him into intercession. In the face of overwhelming and gruesome physical circumstances, his spirit rose up in all of its strength and led him where he otherwise would not have gone. This was not luck, and this was not the ministry of a famous and anointed "man of God"; it was the fruit produced in the life of a normal, everyday believer who lived in constant communion with the Holy Spirit. Because he strengthened his spirit through praying in tongues, in the hour of crisis he was able to access the power of God and call forth a miracle.

EDIFYING OURSELVES

He who speaks in a tongue edifies himself... (1 Corinthians 14:4).

Right after Paul declares to the Corinthians that when they speak in tongues they are speaking mysteries straight to God, he makes another significant statement: *"He who speaks in a tongue edifies himself...."* The subject of edification is central to understanding the glory of speaking in tongues. There are many powerful truths contained in Paul's statement about tongues and edification, and I am going to spend the next two chapters examining each of these truths individually. The first one that I want to look at is the reality that we have been given the gift of tongues in order to strengthen ourselves in the Lord. This is one of the greatest benefits that Paul attributes to speaking in tongues; when we speak in tongues, we are able to personally strengthen our spirits.

We are living in a generation that places great emphasis on physical fitness, health, and body building. I appreciate this because physical health is important, and I am constantly seeking to develop this area of my life. However, the Church today is filled with Christians who may be fit in their bodies, but many times are weak, apathetic, and vulnerable to every attack of the evil one in their spirits. The truth is that if we were as committed to developing our spiritual might as we are our physical might, we would see a revival break out in this nation. God wants to release revival even more than we want it, but He is waiting for us to rise up with spiritual strength and violence and grab hold of Him ourselves.

"And from the days of John the Baptist until now the kingdom of heaven suffers [permits, gives way to] *violence, and the violent take it by force"* (Matt. 11:12). What was true in Jesus' day is true today; the Kingdom is apprehended through spiritual force. In this short sentence written to the Corinthians, Paul gives us the remedy for our weak, impotent Christianity. We must engage the life of the Spirit within through praying in the Spirit.

"He who speaks in a tongue edifies himself...." When we pray in the Spirit, we are not strengthening others; we are strengthening and edifying ourselves. We are actually called to build ourselves up. I love going to conferences and receiving impartations. I love the books, and I love the teaching series, but *nothing can build me up as effectively as praying in the Holy Spirit for extended periods of time.* No teaching or impartation or prophecy can replace the power of my spirit rising up and bringing my mind, will, emotions, and body into alignment with the Holy Spirit as I speak in tongues.

Several years ago there was a highly publicized legal battle concerning a woman in a vegetative state. Her family was fighting in the courts over the decision to remove her feeding tube. In the midst of the media frenzy over this case, the Lord spoke to me one day and said, "I am about to take the Church off of her feeding tube. I am going to teach her how to eat." The truth is that many of us have been on a spiritual feeding tube for so long that we have lost the capacity to sustain true spiritual life on our own. We are living on a machine—surviving off of the second-hand spiritual experiences of our leaders—and we are missing out on the abundant life we are called to in Christ. But God is going to change all that; He is going to teach us how to eat, how to engage the life in our spirits.

The Holy Spirit is calling the Body of Christ individually and corporately to stand as priests and minister to God. You and I have been redeemed to live before God through the sacrifice of Jesus Christ. Jesus forever lives to make intercession, and He has raised us up from death for the purpose of joining with Him in His priestly ministry of intimacy and intercession before God. Through Christ, we have been seated at the right hand of God for the purpose of ministering to Him and partnering with Him. We are partakers of the heavenly calling that is eternal.

But you are a chosen generation, a royal priesthood, a holy nation, His own special people, that you may proclaim the praises of Him who called you out of darkness into His marvelous light (1 Peter 2:9).

We have been brought near before God to declare and to manifest the glorious redemption of Jesus in the Earth. We are called as priests to open up our mouths and stand before God. *And no one can do this for us.* God has a part, and we have a part in this heavenly calling; we cannot do His part, and He will not do ours.

It is with this understanding of our place as ministers before God that praying in tongues takes on such a significant role. I believe that the Lord is raising up a generation who will not only seek His face in a corporate setting with other believers, but who will also meet with Him on their own. So many believers think of the message at church as their main source of spiritual fire. The facts are, if that sermon is our source of fire, then it will mostly be forgotten by Tuesday afternoon. However, if it serves as fuel for our fire, then it will last for decades. We must cultivate communion within our spirits; we must edify ourselves so that when we receive a word or prayer for impartation, it will fuel and expand the fire already burning within us.

First John 2:20 states, *"But you have an anointing from the Holy One, and you know all things."* A few verses later John declares,

But the anointing which you have received from Him abides in you, and you do not need that anyone teach you; but as the same anointing teaches you concerning all things, and is true, and is not a lie, and just as it has taught you, you will abide in Him (1 John 2:27).

These two verses state that within every believer is the anointing of the Holy Spirit, and this anointing teaches us all things.

In other words, the things we hear from our leaders will actually confirm the very things the Holy Spirit is already speaking to us. We will have a living witness in our spirits when we listen to prophets, pastors, and teachers. The very purpose of these gifts in the Body is to add fuel to the existing realities of communion, understanding, and revelation that are flowing in our spirits from the anointing dwelling in us.

Jude addresses this same truth in his famous passage on praying in the Spirit. In verse 3 he says,

> *Beloved, while I was very diligent to write to you concerning our common salvation, I found it necessary to write to you exhorting you to contend earnestly for the faith which was once for all delivered to the saints.*

The charge we are given is to contend earnestly for the faith. Many of us see phrases like "contend," or "wage war," and we really don't know what that looks like. Fortunately, Jude tells us how to do this in verses 20-21:

> *But you, beloved, building yourselves up on your most holy faith, praying in the Holy Spirit, keep yourselves in the love of God, looking for the mercy of our Lord Jesus Christ unto eternal life.*

We see here that the way to increase and grow in the original faith that was given through Jesus is by praying in the Spirit, praying in tongues. Note the use of the word *yourselves;* Jude challenges us to enter into our priestly calling and build ourselves up. He is saying, "God is not going to do it for you; you must build yourself up." We have a responsibility to edify ourselves by praying in the Spirit.

If we are honest, many of us would admit that we are living defeated lives because our spirits are weak. We are powerless to resist the enemy because we are allowing our emotions, our appetites, and our circumstances to run our lives. We are led by how we feel and what we think—by everything but the Holy Spirit. But God is saying, "I want you to build a building: your life is this building, the temple of the Holy Spirit. And I want you to build it on your most holy faith by praying in the Holy Spirit." When we build ourselves up through engaging the power and life of God by speaking in tongues, we will begin to find ourselves walking victoriously in the Spirit. This is the same charge that Paul gave to the Corinthians when he told them that he who speaks in a tongue edifies himself. Isn't it glorious and freeing to our hearts to know that we don't need an apostle or prophet to lay hands on us? We can lay hands on ourselves and call forth the life of God within us as we pray in the Spirit.

"Do not send me any more messengers." So wrote John of the Cross, a Spanish mystic of the sixteenth century. In his poem, *Spiritual Canticle*, John wrote of the deep love of the soul for Jesus as the love between a bride and bridegroom. In the above quotation, the soul declares that it will only be satisfied with direct communion. "Do not send me any more messengers." Have we touched the place of love and longing where we cease to be content with messengers who receive the Word of God for us? Are we ready to cry out for direct communion with God?

The Need for Strength

We have looked at the responsibility we have been given to build ourselves up individually and personally. Now let's look at what it actually means to do so—what it means to *edify* ourselves. The *21st Century Lexicon* offers two basic definitions of this word. First, *edification* is the building up, establishing, or strengthening of a person or institution. Second, *edification* is the building or construction of a physical structure.[2] Both of these definitions apply to the experience and results of praying in the Spirit, so we will examine both in detail.

Let's look at the idea of strengthening first. I like to use the analogy of charging a battery when I describe what happens to our spirits as we strengthen them through speaking in tongues. If a battery in an automobile runs down, we hook it up to a power source and charge it up. In other words, we build up the battery until it has the power to do what it was made to do. The same thing happens in the spirit when we speak in tongues: we are charging our battery—our spirits—in order to release the Word of God with power. As believers we have the power of the eternal God living inside of us. When we engage His life through speaking in tongues, we receive that very power in our mind, will, emotions, and body.

Our spirits are designed to be the power source of our lives, and where our spirits go, our souls and our bodies will follow. This means that when we speak in tongues, we are actually training our spirits in getting breakthrough. In Romans 8, Paul writes that the same Spirit that raised Christ from the dead dwells in us, and just as the Spirit gives life to our spirits, He will also give life to our mortal bodies (see Rom. 8:10-11). In other words, the body is subject to the spirit. If we want to see breakthrough in our lives, we need to strengthen and train our spirits until our souls and bodies are brought into alignment under the leadership of the Holy Spirit and we begin to run on divine strength. I love this reality because we are given the glory of strengthening ourselves; we have been given everything we need to build up our spirits so that they lead us into holiness (see 2 Pet. 1:3). We have the power to strengthen our minds, our wills, and our emotions for righteousness. Proverbs 16:32 says that *"he who rules his spirit [is better] than he who takes a city"*; in other words, in God's eyes, it is better for us to train and rule our spirits than to expand our influence in the natural!

As the director of the Forerunner Program at IHOPU (International House of Prayer University), I am in contact with thousands of young adults. I have observed that one of the greatest obstacles that must be overcome in the training of the next generation is the weakness of their spirits. They do not know how to build themselves up. This is a generation that is driven by their circumstances and emotions; they base their actions entirely on how they feel. As a result, many young believers reject the labor and discipline necessary to attain spiritual maturity because such labor is uncomfortable and inconvenient. I believe that one of the greatest gods in our culture is the god of convenience. We are a generation given to the pursuit of ease and comfort. But God is the same yesterday, today, and tomorrow; He never changes, and we won't find Him at a McDonald's drive-through. I have found that when students grasp this reality and begin to pray in the Spirit for extended periods of time over the course of months and even years, their emotions are gradually transformed by the strength of God, and they become unshakeable in their faith.

I believe that God is raising up a John the Baptist generation that will prepare the Earth for the second coming of Jesus in the same way that John prepared the nation of Israel in the first century. In Luke 1:80, we are given a significant insight into John's preparation for ministry: *"So the child grew and became strong in spirit, and was in the deserts till the day of his manifestation to Israel."* This phrase *became strong in spirit* has gripped me as I consider its implications. The strength that I see most frequently manifested in my own life and in the Church is strength of soul, not strength of spirit. The cry of my heart is to see a generation arise that is strong in spirit.

This type of strength is only cultivated over time. *We must make daily decisions to swim against the current of our emotions and our mindsets—to be led by the Spirit rather than the flesh.* Any personal trainer or body builder will tell you that strength is built through resistance. And strength of spirit is built in the same way: through resistance. As we learn to press against the pull of our emotions, bodies, and circumstances, we begin to grow in strength and receive power to walk in spiritual breakthrough and stand steady during difficult seasons.

The Holy Spirit is highlighting the "Spirit of Elijah" in the Body of Christ these days. We are also hearing about the "double portion" that fell on Elisha and how God is releasing a double portion of the Spirit that was on Elijah. The thing that I love about the Elijah/Elisha story is that when Elijah met Elisha, Elisha was plowing his field with 12 oxen! (See 1 Kings 19:19.) I believe that the "double portion" is received in the context of plowing our fields, which is our own personal lives, interior lives, preparing ourselves for the commissioning of God.

As I have stated in earlier chapters, the majority of believers live from crisis to crisis, running to and fro and never truly getting breakthrough. However, as we tap into the reservoir of power in our spirits through speaking in tongues, we will strengthen and train ourselves to bring the life of our souls (mind, will, and emotions) and the pull of our flesh under the leadership of the Holy Spirit.

Look at what the Book of James says concerning the power of our speech:

> *If anyone does not stumble in word, he is a perfect man, able also to bridle the whole body. Indeed, we put bits in horses' mouths that they may obey us, and we turn their whole body. Look also at ships: although they are*

> *so large and are driven by fierce winds, they are turned*
> *by a very small rudder wherever the pilot desires. Even*
> *so the tongue is a little member and boasts great things*
> (James 3:2b-5a).

In the same way that a small rudder directs the course of a mighty ship, so our tongues direct the course of our spiritual lives. Though James does not directly reference the gift of tongues, I believe that when we pray in the Spirit we are actually bringing the rest of our members underneath the leadership of God. This is true internal power and strength.

If you are struggling with negative thought patterns, if you are dealing with anger or jealousy or self-hatred, begin to pray in the spirit and speak the Word of God over yourself and then watch the enemy flee.

Jackie Pullinger is a missionary and evangelist who has been ministering in Hong Kong since 1966. In the early days of her ministry, she specifically worked with the gang members, prostitutes, and drug addicts who lived in the portion of Hong Kong known as the Walled City. It was during that period of her life that she discovered the power of tongues to free men and women from their dependence on heroin and opium. In her book, *Chasing the Dragon,* she shares many stories of addicts who were miraculously delivered through praying in the Spirit. After relating the testimony of Ah Kei, a heroin addict for ten years with a hundred-dollar-a-day habit who withdrew painlessly in less than a week, Jackie Pullinger says this:

> If he experienced any twinge of pain, we would
> quickly urge him to pray in tongues, and the pain
> would miraculously disappear. *Now we knew without*
> *a shadow of doubt that praying in the Spirit was the*
> *answer for painless withdrawal from heroin.*[3]

A little later she writes,

> Word quickly spread along the addict grapevine that
> if they were willing to believe in Jesus, they would
> receive some kind of power that enabled them to kick
> drugs painlessly....As each boy arrived, the miracle
> was repeated: He came to Christ and came off drugs
> painlessly when he prayed in the language of the
> Spirit.[4]

I do not think the Body of Christ fully realizes the power of bringing the body and soul into submission under the spirit—a power that breaks physical addictions and strongholds and sets the captives free.

I want to emphasize again that the strength I am talking about is not strength of personality; it isn't based on gifting or intelligence. John the Baptist went into the wilderness to become "strong in spirit." There was a divine transaction that occurred in the desert as he traded his natural strengths and abilities for the resources of Heaven. So often in the Church we see people who have larger-than-life, highly charismatic personalities, and we mistake this for strength of spirit. We judge people based on their physical, mental, and emotional capabilities, but strength of soul and strength of spirit are two different things. A person can be incredibly quiet, gentle, and shy, yet possess the spirit of a mighty warrior.

A strong spirit is what enables us to stay silent when we are being attacked and criticized; it produces patience and perfect peace in the midst of disaster; it carries the authority to break the power of demons with the Word of God; it produces self-control. Jesus displayed true strength of spirit when He slept in the midst of a raging storm that threatened to capsize the disciples' boat (see Matt. 8:24). A mighty spirit is a spirit rooted and grounded in the

Lord, confident and content in every situation. Paul touched this transcendent power when he wrote to the Philippians, *"I can do all things through Christ who strengthens me"* (Phil. 4:13). The strength of God was evident not only in Paul's character, but also in his ministry. In Acts it says that supernatural healing was released by handkerchiefs and aprons that Paul had touched (see Acts 19:11-12). How many mighty spirits are there in the Body today?

Praying in the Spirit will increase the Spirit of might within us. We will receive power from on high as we strengthen ourselves through speaking in tongues. Not only will our ability to choose righteousness increase, but our ability to wield the Word of God— the sword of the Spirit—will increase in power also. In Ephesians 6, right after Paul charges the believers to take up the sword of the Spirit, he tells them to pray always in the Spirit (see Eph. 6:17-18). Praying in the Spirit strengthens and trains us to wield the sword of the Spirit with power and precision. It is strength of spirit coupled with a life in the Word of God that releases an explosion of the Kingdom when we speak, when we preach, when we serve, when we prophesy, when we lay hands on the sick. We are called to receive the strength and power of God in our spirits every day. As I stated earlier, many believers are walking around looking like Arnold Schwarzenegger in the natural, but their spirits are on life support. The sword of the Spirit is the most powerful weapon in existence, yet so many are trying to wield William Wallace's sword with a Minnie Mouse spirit.

The reason that the Scriptures exhort us to strengthen and edify ourselves is because we do not have the strength we need on our own: *"for without Me you can do nothing"* (John 15:5c). Every day we are in desperate need of a divine transference; we must use all of our strength to receive all of His. There isn't a single battle that we are called to fight in our own strength— not one. *"'Not by might nor by power, but by My Spirit,' says the*

Lord of hosts" (Zech. 4:6b). We are always called to strengthen our spirits in the Lord. When David was in the midst of one of the darkest times of his life, facing mutiny from his men and defeat at the hands of his enemies, the Scripture says that he strengthened himself in the Lord (see 1 Sam. 30:6). When Paul wrote to the church in Ephesus regarding spiritual warfare (which we will look at more closely in a later chapter), he made it very clear that believers were called to stand in God's strength. *"Finally, my brethren, be strong in the Lord and in the power of His might"* (Eph. 6:10). Before we even begin to equip ourselves with the armor of God, we are called to stand in His strength. This is the prerequisite for Christian warfare.

And this is why speaking in tongues is imperative. When we pray in the Spirit, we are building ourselves up in our most holy faith; we are strengthening ourselves by the Holy Spirit and trading our strength for His. As we engage the Holy Spirit through tongues, we draw from the power and resources of God dwelling within our spirits, and we receive the very might of God. I picture an oil rig drilling in the Earth, going back and forth as it pulls the oil up from beneath the surface. When I pray in tongues, I see my tongue going down into the depths of my spirit and pulling up the life of God into my soul.

We have lived too long without this glorious reality. The might of God is ours in the Spirit, and we continue to live without it because of the means by which He releases that might and because we are under the delusion that God will do everything for us; we want God to transform us without ever having to engage the resources He has given us. We stumble over God's ways, and so we continue to live mostly in defeat. Yet for those who resolve with great faith and spiritual violence to contend for breakthrough in their lives by praying in tongues, the life and power of God will not fail to be released in increasing measure.

The writer of Hebrews exhorts us in chapter 10: *"For you have need of endurance, so that after you have done the will of God, you may receive the promise"* (Heb. 10:36). Paul tells the Ephesians no less than four times to stand as he writes to them about spiritual warfare (see Eph. 6:10-18). The message of these two passages is the same: the breakthrough will come, but we are in need of endurance. We need divine strength and might in our spirits to stand, to resist, to fight, and to declare the will of God in the Earth.

This is what Paul prayed for the Church in Ephesians 3: *"that He would grant you, according to the riches of His glory, to be strengthened with might through His Spirit in the inner man"* (Eph. 3:16). It is through the Spirit of God that we are strengthened and the fullness of God is released in our lives. Notice that the Lord strengthens us *"according to the riches of His glory"*; this is a key phrase. Our God is rich; we cannot fathom the wealth of resources that He has placed in us through His Spirit. I like to use the analogy of an ATM. We have been given the riches of God in our inner selves; we have a billion dollars in our bellies, but we must use our ATM cards to access the money. We must use the language of the Spirit to access the Spirit and the riches of His glory. Have we begun to fathom the treasury of God's glorious riches? When Paul prayed this prayer for the Ephesians, he was asking God to deposit the treasures of Heaven in their account by the Holy Spirit. He was asking for a holy transference of God's glory into the depths of our inner person.

Our need is for the release of the ministry of the Spirit within us. As the Spirit touches our inner person, we are empowered and strengthened to live as we ought.

> *He gives power to the weak, and to those who have*
> *no might He increases strength. Even the youths shall*
> *faint and be weary, and the young men shall utterly*

fall, but those who wait on the Lord shall renew their strength; they shall mount up with wings like eagles, they shall run and not be weary, they shall walk and not faint (Isaiah 40:29-31).

Our focus and concern must be on how to consistently receive increasing amounts of the life of the Spirit. This is why praying in tongues is so crucial. Praying in tongues strengthens and prepares our spirits for greater manifestations of the life of Christ in us. When we edify ourselves through speaking in tongues, we pray the mind of the Spirit, asking Him to come and release His glory and strength into our depths so that we may grow in our knowledge of God.

ENDNOTES

1. Shelley Hundley, "Transformation and the Four Forms of Prayer," lecture (Kansas City, MO: IHOPU, February 10, 2011).

2. Dictionary.com's *21st Century Lexicon*, s.v. "Edify"; http://dictionary .reference.com/browse/edify; (accessed June 30, 2011).

3. Jackie Pullinger, *Chasing the Dragon* (Ventura, CA: Gospel Light, 1980), 149.

4. Ibid., 154, 157.

Chapter 6

BUILDING A CAPACITY FOR GOD

As stated in the last chapter, the definition of edification is related to the idea of strengthening our spirits. It is also related to the idea of building our spirits. In the original Greek, the word *edify* literally means "to erect a building or construct a house." This language gives us a powerful word picture of praying in the Spirit; when we speak in tongues, we are building within our spirits a house where we can experience communion with God. We are actually increasing our capacity to contain the glory of the Holy Spirit.

The call to edification is the call to build ourselves. Today the Church is consumed with building platforms and influence; our ministries have grown large, but our hearts have grown small. We have spent our time and energy on external realities and have neglected the building of our inner selves. I believe that the Lord is releasing a prophetic call to the Body of Christ, and it is an exhortation to edification. If we begin to build ourselves, then the Lord will watch over our spheres of influence. The Body of

Christ has traded depth for width; we have become horizontally focused at the expense of cultivating interior realities and at the expense of our lives, our marriages, and our families. For too long we have focused only on what we can see, but there is an entire world alive inside of us.

One of my favorite songs is written by a worship leader here at the House of Prayer, Misty Edwards. In this song she describes the human soul as a garden surrounded by walls, a garden that only God can access. Most of our true living takes place "behind the face," in the depths of our souls where we are alone with the Holy Spirit.

> *You've hedged me in*
> *With skin all around me*
> *I'm a garden enclosed*
> *A locked garden*
> *Life takes place behind the face*
>
> *Where it's You and me alone, God*
> *Here it's You and me alone*
> *Here it's You and me alone, God*
> *You and me alone*
> *I don't want to waste my life*
> *Living on the outside*
> *I'm going to live from the inside out*
> *I don't want to waste my time*
> *Living on the outside*
> *I'm going to live from the inside out* [1]

This is why it is so important to understand the way that God has designed us. We are spirit, soul, and body; the body houses the eternal reality—the spirit—and this is the reality that we must build.

In His last public discourse, Jesus told a parable related to this issue. He introduced us to two types of ministries that will emerge at the end of the age; one He called foolish and the other He called wise.

> *Then the kingdom of heaven shall be likened to ten virgins who took their lamps and went out to meet the bridegroom. Now five of them were wise, and five were foolish. Those who were foolish took their lamps and took no oil with them, but the wise took oil in their vessels with their lamps. But while the bridegroom was delayed, they all slumbered and slept.*
>
> *And at midnight a cry was heard: "Behold, the bridegroom is coming; go out to meet him!" Then all those virgins arose and trimmed their lamps. And the foolish said to the wise, "Give us some of your oil, for our lamps are going out." But the wise answered, saying, "No, lest there should not be enough for us and you; but go rather to those who sell, and buy for yourselves." And while they went to buy, the bridegroom came, and those who were ready went in with him to the wedding; and the door was shut.*
>
> *Afterward the other virgins came also, saying, "Lord, Lord, open to us!" But he answered and said, "Assuredly, I say to you, I do not know you"* (Matthew 25:1-12).

The difference between the wise and foolish virgins is this: the wise prioritized the size of their hearts over the size of their ministries, while the foolish did the reverse. The wise virgins spent time building their interior life in God and cultivating intimacy and communion—in other words, they stored up oil. For a season they appeared foolish because the growth of their hearts came at the expense of their external reputation, ministry, and success. But though their spheres of influence were smaller, these wise ones were building up their hearts in the secret place. The foolish virgins, on the other hand, spent time building their external circumstances. They appeared more successful until the prophetic season shifted. Then, when the cry, *"Behold, the bridegroom is coming; go out to meet him!"* was heard, the foolish virgins, who were busy managing their public platforms, received a revelation of the bankruptcy of their interior lives. In that hour, however, the wise virgins who had prioritized their hearts came forward from the place of hiddenness to the place of leadership in the Body of Christ.

I believe that as we approach the last days we will see this shift take place; in fact, it has already begun, and it is going to increase. God is going to take people like David—those who have cultivated a history in God during seasons of obscurity, who have experienced breakthroughs in the areas of shame, rejection, and fear, and who have drawn closer to Christ—and place them in positions of authority over nations.

David's victory over the lions and bears in the wilderness of Bethlehem qualified him to shepherd the people of Israel. Though he was overlooked by his own family, when the season shifted and Israel was threatened by Goliath, David showed up with supernatural boldness, authority, anointing, and clarity: *"...who is this uncircumcised Philistine, that he should defy the armies of the living God?"* (1 Sam. 17:26). I believe that God is going to raise up a generation that will take on the end-time Goliath—the antichrist—with the same power and authority. They will be delivered from the need for stages and platforms and will be wholly fulfilled in ministering to an audience of One. Therefore, God will entrust them with the fullness of His anointing, His power, and His life.

This reality applies not only to individuals, but also to organizations. I believe that we will see many mega-ministries go from the front to the back of the line overnight. It isn't only the big ministries that neglect the call to edification, though. There are many small ministries that despise their lack of influence and can never seem to get over it. Because of this, they do not cultivate and expand the size of their hearts, and their spiritual bankruptcy will be exposed in the hour of crisis.

The spiritual strength and depth of God's champions will be revealed as well, but it is not a strength that will appear magically (and conveniently) in that hour. Before we are commissioned to prepare the way of the Lord, we must first prepare ourselves by allowing God to refine our hearts and increase their capacity. Many men and women seek prominent positions of leadership without embracing the season of preparation. Then, when they achieve what they were striving for, they discover that they lack the capacity to handle it. This is when character flaws, scandals, breakdowns, and burnouts erupt in the Church.

"He who speaks in a tongue edifies himself..." If we want to avoid the pain of spiritual bankruptcy and brokenness, we must dedicate ourselves to enlarging the capacity of our hearts and engaging the life of the Spirit through extended periods of speaking in tongues. This is what will enable us to bear the burden of leadership when it comes along. However, the process of preparation is a painful one; as we give ourselves to praying in the Spirit, we will find that the Lord is committed to uprooting every false foundation and false identity within. He will tear down every definition of success that is not rooted in Christ because He wants to build a dwelling place in the spirit, by the Spirit.

PREPARE THE WAY OF THE LORD

Look at how Isaiah describes the work of preparation: *"... Build up, build up the highway! Take out the stones, lift up a banner for the peoples!"* (Isa. 62:10). The prophet describes this same process in an earlier passage:

> *Prepare the way of the Lord; make straight in the desert a highway for our God. Every valley shall be exalted and every mountain and hill brought low; the crooked places shall be made straight and the rough places smooth* (Isaiah 40:3b-4).

These verses refer to the practice in the ancient world of constructing and improving the main road into a city in preparation for the arrival of a king. Laborers would remove stones, erect bridges, and level the uneven ground so that the king's entrance into the city would be swift and unhindered.

According to Isaiah, one of the first tasks in the edification process is the preparation of the ground through the removing of stones (fear, rejection, shame, and insecurity) and the leveling of the high places (pride, idolatry, and self-sufficiency). In other words, before we can build a dwelling place for God in our spirits, we must cooperate with the Holy Spirit to tear down every false foundation in our souls. Have you ever watched a home makeover show? I have seen many amazing homes constructed, but I have never seen a new structure built on top of an existing one. Before they build a new house, they have to take a wrecking ball and destroy the old house. *Speaking in tongues, paired with a life in the Word of God, releases the wrecking ball of the Spirit in our souls; as we persevere in prayer, the Holy Spirit tears down, uproots, and destroys everything in us that is not conducive to the life of God and everything that is not aligned with His holiness. This is not a* fun process, but I would rather cooperate with God as He exposes and destroys corrupt structures in my life now, than wait until the day when I stand before Him and my entire life is tested by His fire.

> *You are God's building. According to the grace of God which was given to me, as a wise master builder I have laid the foundation, and another builds on it. But let each one take heed how he builds on it. For no other foundation can anyone lay than that which is laid, which is Jesus Christ. Now if anyone builds on this foundation with gold, silver, precious stones, wood, hay, straw, each one's work will become clear; for the Day will declare it, because it will be revealed by fire; and the fire will test each one's work, of what sort it is. If anyone's work which he has built on it endures, he will receive a reward. If anyone's work is burned, he will suffer loss; but he himself will be saved, yet so as through fire.*
>
> *Do you not know that you are the temple of God and that the Spirit of God dwells in you? If anyone defiles the temple of God, God will destroy him. For the temple of God is holy, which temple you are* (1 Corinthians 3:9c-17).

The edification process is a painful process because God is destroying the existing building in our souls for the purpose of raising a new structure. There must be a breaking up of the fallow ground before the power of fellowshipping with the Spirit is felt. In Hosea 10:12 the prophet commands the people of God to break up their fallow ground; just as a farmer must first break and till the ground before he plants the seed, so we must prepare the soil of our hearts for impartation from God. Many of us think that when we begin to pray in the Spirit we are going to automatically enter into glorious realms. The Lord may allow us to have that experience initially in order to hook us, but there will come a time when He begins to deal with the existing state of our souls.

This can knock people off track if they aren't expecting it. A friend of mine experienced a season where, whenever he prayed in the Spirit, God would highlight areas of sin and compromise in his life. We must truly settle it in our hearts that we are committed to persevering, no matter how uncomfortable we are. I have found that it is very common for my mind to be filled with distracting and wandering thoughts when I begin to speak in tongues. Not only will I have to battle thoughts such as, *I could be doing something better with my time,* or *This is useless,* but often as I continue to pray, impurities will begin to rise to the surface. We may find that thoughts or images related to fear, lust, anger, and so forth will enter our minds. But we must not be discouraged by this. When we are faced with this reality, we must remember that we are fellowshipping with God and that He is removing the dross of our unrenewed minds. We can thank the Holy Spirit for the work of cleansing that He is doing even as we take authority over those thoughts and images and cast them down.

When I think about the work of preparing my spirit to be the temple of God, I picture my tongue like a jackhammer that is breaking the rocks into pieces and removing everything that is hindering the flow of the life of God in me. As believers, we are called to prepare the way of the Lord; we are called to build a structure to house His activity and leadership in our lives. Speaking in tongues is a ministry of preparation and building; it removes the stones that hinder the life of God, and it enlarges our capacity to house the work of the Spirit. This ministry is violent in nature, and so we must set our minds and hearts to persevere until we achieve breakthrough.

Once we have established the expectation that praying in the Spirit will uproot the darkness in our souls, we will begin to experience incremental breakthroughs of the Holy Spirit in our minds, wills, emotions, and bodies. These breakthroughs may not manifest immediately, however. After all, it takes time to build up walls of resistance against the Spirit, so we should expect it to take time to deconstruct those walls. Even on a daily basis, it takes around 20 minutes of praying in the Spirit before I begin to consciously receive breakthrough from God. For those initial 20 minutes, I am usually battling my wandering thoughts and constantly bringing my mind back to the focal points found in Scripture. However, after about 20 minutes, I usually find that my spiritual perception is awakened, and I begin to hear and receive from God. I very rarely "feel" like praying in tongues when I begin, but I've developed a history of persevering and experiencing the fruit of breakthrough, and I am confident that I will continue to reap amazing benefits in the long run. I don't have life-changing encounters every day, but over time I have found that my life is increasingly fueled by the life and strength of Heaven. One of the greatest things that I've been trained in through praying in the Spirit is breakthrough. The Lord is training a generation to experience breakthrough in their souls and see the life of God break forth out of them.

GROWING INTO FULLNESS

Edification is not only about growth; it is about fullness and the preparation for the glory of God. This is the purpose behind our growth: we are not satisfied with the mere edges of the knowledge of God or with a casual relationship with Christ, but we want to grow up internally and spiritually into complete union with the head of the Church, Jesus (see Eph. 4:15). We long to be transformed into the very image and character of Christ.

We were made for the fullness of eternal union with God. Right now, Christ is in Heaven and the Body is on Earth; yet through the ministry of the Holy Spirit we are joined together. And we are growing up into the head until the two realms become one. This is the ultimate goal of our edification.

In Ephesians Paul prays that Christ would dwell in our hearts by faith:

> *That Christ may dwell in your hearts through faith; that you, being rooted and grounded in love, may be able to comprehend with all the saints what is the width and length and depth and height—to know the love of Christ which passes knowledge; that you may be filled with all the fullness of God* (Ephesians 3:17-19).

Paul is casting a vision for fullness in this passage; he does not want believers to be satisfied with occasional encounters. We were not made to only feel the presence of the Lord on Sunday mornings. We were made to contain the constant and abiding presence of Jesus. He wants to dwell in our hearts. Paul was touching the reality of the fullness of the baptism of the Spirit and connecting it to the need to build and prepare our spirits for that baptism. We must be strengthened with might, and our walls must be fortified before we can become the dwelling place of God. The word *dwell* means "to settle down and remain." This is the goal of our faith and the picture of fullness in the life of the believer: unhindered and abiding union with Christ.

It is important to remember that Paul did not pray this for unbelievers; he desired for Christ to dwell in the hearts of believers. We were made to know the dimensions of God; we were made for the realm of the width, the length, the depth, the height. We were meant to experience it—not just know about it, but know it in a deep and intimate way. When I set my soul to wait on the Lord as I speak in tongues, or pray quietly in the Spirit as I read the Word of God, I am making room for the fullness of God to take up residence in my inner person. I am preparing my heart for communion and creating space within my soul for God to be with me. *"If anyone loves Me, he will keep My word; and My Father will love him and We will come to him and make Our home with him"* (John 14:23).

Praying in the Spirit not only creates space within us for the life of God, but it builds and strengthens the connection between our spirits and God. Remember the definition of *edification* in the original Greek? When we edify ourselves we are literally building a house. In Genesis 28, Jacob had a vision of the house of God. The vision began with a ladder being established on the Earth and reaching to Heaven. Then Heaven opened and the angels of God began to ascend and descend. When Jacob awoke, he called the place *Bethel,* which means "house of God." In other words, Jacob understood that the place where Heaven and Earth were connected was the place of God's habitation. Jesus pointed to this reality when He told the disciples that they would see Heaven open and the angels ascending and descending upon Him (see John 1:51). He made it clear that He was Jacob's ladder. When we speak in tongues, we are building a ladder from Earth to Heaven and are connecting to Christ. We are building something to contain the atmosphere and activity of the supernatural realm. And just like Jacob, we can call this edifice, this ladder connecting us to our heavenly home, the house of God.

The more that we set our hearts to connect with the realities of Heaven, the more those realities will abide within us experientially. I often find that, after praying in tongues for 20 or 30 minutes, small measures of the glory of Heaven begin to manifest in my spirit and in my senses. The heavens seem to, in a small measure, open over my life, and I experience the realm of angelic activity and the realm of encounter. Though this is only a small foretaste of eternity, these moments of communion are real and priceless—and they are available to all believers who build their spirits in the place of prayer. *"Heaven is My throne, and earth is My footstool. Where is the house that you will build Me?"* (Isa. 66:1). God is longing for a place to dwell, and He is looking for men and women to give priority to communion and to build a place of encounter within their spirits.

EDIFICATION AND UNITY

You also, as living stones, are being built up a spiritual house, a holy priesthood, to offer up spiritual sacrifices acceptable to God through Jesus Christ (1 Peter 2:5).

We have spent a lot of time emphasizing the personal benefits of praying in the Spirit. The gift of tongues isn't only about individual edification; it is about corporate edification. I am convinced that speaking in tongues will serve as one of the primary catalysts for the restoration of apostolic Christianity. One of the key characteristics of the apostolic is building—not building networks or programs, but building and equipping people. Paul himself described the apostolic ministry as analogous to building, and throughout the New Testament we see this connection between building and the apostolic mandate. True apostolic ministry is the building up of the Body in the unity of the Spirit.

And He Himself gave some to be apostles, some prophets, some evangelists, and some pastors and teachers, for the equipping of the saints for the work of ministry, for the edifying [building up] of the body of Christ, till we all come to the unity of the faith and of the knowledge of the Son of God, to a perfect man, to the

> *measure of the stature of the fullness of Christ* (Ephesians 4:11-13).

Building and *unity* are synonymous throughout Scripture. People have tried to achieve unity in their own might and strength many times—the tower of Babel is one of the clearest examples of this. In Genesis 11 we read that all of humankind had one language and they were set on building a city connecting Heaven and Earth so that they could make a name for themselves. It is amazing to consider how much they understood about the power of uniting the natural and spiritual realms. God took the power of their unity so seriously that He actually came down to see the city and the tower they were constructing. And God declared that because they had one language and were united in their efforts to build, nothing they attempted would be withheld from them (see Gen. 11:6). Then the Lord confused their language so that they did not understand one another, and they stopped building. It was when they were no longer of one mind and one language that they stopped building. The legacy of the tower of Babel was not destroyed, though: Babylon, which has served as the antithesis of Jerusalem throughout redemptive history, has its foundations in Babel.

It is interesting to note that, at the end of the age, the Earth is going to see a false unity movement built around the rallying cries of peace and safety and tolerance—a false unity movement with the spirit of Babylon behind it. At the same time, a true restoration of apostolic unity founded on the Spirit of prayer will arise in the Earth. It is also interesting to note that the Lord named the place *Babel* when He confused the language of the earth and scattered the people. Today we use the word *babble* to describe foolish, inarticulate, and incoherent sounds. But on the Day of Pentecost, God used the babblings of tongues to begin building His own structure: the Church. While God chose to use babblings to confuse and scatter the people at Babel, He chose to use babblings once again to release spiritual unity and the testimony of Jesus amongst the believers and to open the heavens over the early Church.

"You also are being built together for a dwelling place of God in the Spirit" (Eph. 2:22). I believe we are going to see a return to apostolic Christianity as we approach the second coming of Jesus. Individual edification ultimately produces corporate edification. As I build me and you build you, together we are built up into the habitation of God in the Spirit. The more we, individually, develop extended times of praying in the Spirit, the more we will see corporate breakthrough, an increase of anointing on the Body, and the fruit of connection between Heaven and Earth. I'm convinced that as we begin to build personal histories of praying in the Spirit for extended periods of time, we will release unity in our marriages, families, churches, and businesses. This is how the Lord builds.

One of the clearest prophetic statements concerning the end-time Church is found in Revelation 22:17—*"And the Spirit and the bride say, 'Come!'..."* At the end of the age, the Holy Spirit and the Church will be fully united in their purpose and desire. The things that are burning in the Holy Spirit will become the very things burning in the heart of the Church. The main agenda of the Holy Spirit is the second coming of Jesus; He desires for the fullness of the plans and purposes of God to come to fruition through the final redemption of all creation. For the past 2,000 years, the Church has been disconnected from this work of the Spirit, but there is coming a day when the Holy Spirit and the Church will operate in profound unity. The heartbeat of Heaven will become the heartbeat of Earth, there will be a united outpouring of intercession birthed from the place of love and communion with the Spirit, and it will culminate in the literal return of Jesus and the reunion of Heaven and Earth. The earth's deep will call out to Heaven's deep and we will see an explosion of light and power manifested at the coming of Jesus.

On the night of His betrayal and arrest, Jesus interceded for coming generations of believers.

> *I do not pray for these alone, but also for those who will believe in Me through their word; that they all may be one, as You, Father, are in Me, and I in You; that they also may be one in Us, that the world may believe that You sent Me* (John 17:20-21).

It has always been the plan of God to release the power of the Spirit and the testimony of Jesus through the unity of His Church, and I am convinced that praying in the Spirit will be a significant catalyst for this unity. As we fellowship with the Holy Spirit and enter into His thoughts, His emotions, and His plans, we will also enter into agreement with one another. From this place of unity, the Bride will cry out with the Holy Spirit for the soon return of her Bridegroom.

ENDNOTE

1. Misty Edwards, "Garden," *Relentless,* Audio CD (Oasis House, 2007).

Chapter 7

LEARNING HOW
TO FIGHT

My friend loves to share the story of one of his first experiences with deliverance. He was attending seminary at the time and a professor invited him along with a few other students to participate in a time of deliverance ministry as intercessors. They were supposed to sit on the far side of the room and pray in the Spirit while the professor ministered to the individual. Well, as he and his fellow students began to speak in tongues quietly, the demons started manifesting. The man was thrown to the ground and started yelling at the intercessors to stop praying. My friend was terrified! His professor, however, commanded the demons in the name of Jesus to interpret what was being spoken in tongues. In a voice clearly not his own, the man hissed, "They are declaring the victory of Jesus." Greatly encouraged by this, the students began to pray in the Spirit with greater confidence (and volume). Again the man yelled at them to stop, and again the professor commanded the demons to interpret the tongues. "They are prophesying our coming demise," the man hissed.

This experience convinced my friend of the power of praying in tongues in the midst of spiritual warfare.

It was the reality of spiritual warfare that first propelled me into the practice of praying in tongues for extended periods of time. When my family first moved to Kansas City to join IHOP, we entered into a season of constant warfare. If it wasn't one thing, it was something else—the baby was sick, or we experienced tormenting dreams at night, or there was unusual strife in the house— and I didn't know what to do to break the cycle. In frustration, I would pace throughout our apartment praying loudly in tongues until I began to feel peace in my own spirit and in the household. Sometimes this only took 20 minutes, and sometimes it took two hours, but in the process I learned to discern the presence of breakthrough. At the end of that season, I realized that I had unwittingly stumbled upon a powerful truth related to tongues: praying in the Spirit is a weapon of war. The Lord was teaching me the power of warring in the spirit in those early days, and I believe that He is going to arm His Church with this revelation on a global scale before He returns.

At the end of the age, spiritual warfare will reach unprecedented levels. Revelation 12 describes the period in human history when the prayers of the saints cast satan out of the second heavens.

> *And war broke out in heaven: Michael and his angels fought with the dragon; and the dragon and his angels fought, but they did not prevail, nor was a place found for them in heaven any longer. So the great dragon was cast out, that serpent of old, called the Devil and Satan, who deceives the whole world; he was cast to the earth, and his angels were cast out with him.... "Therefore rejoice, O heavens, and you who dwell in them! Woe to the inhabitants of the earth and the*

sea! For the devil has come down to you, having great wrath, because he knows that he has a short time" (Revelation 12:7-9,12).

Humanity will experience one of the greatest transitions in redemptive history as the devil falls from his place of authority in the heavens and stages his final battle campaign here on Earth through the reign of the antichrist. We are not yet living in those last days, but I am convinced that we are closer than we realize and that even now the Lord is taking His Church through spiritual boot camp to prepare them for the days ahead. David said that it was God who trained his hands for battle and his fingers for war (see Ps. 144:1). We are in a war right now in the spirit, and we must awaken to this reality before the fighting intensifies and overwhelms us.

The day we said yes to Jesus, two things happened: we were enlisted in an army, and we became targets of the kingdom of darkness. If we do not approach our spiritual walks with this understanding then we will set ourselves up for defeat. Knowing that we are in a war and that participation is not optional will forearm us and help us to walk in victory as Christians. Too many believers do not take the battle seriously, but beloved, there is a real war with a real enemy seeking to devour us. He is looking for weak, powerless people who place their confidence in the flesh and are naïve when it comes to the things of the Spirit.

We desperately need a fresh revelation of the warfare of the believer. The lack of this revelation has left us vulnerable to the schemes of the enemy. We need to realize that we were made to come alive and discover God as we fight and contend and wrestle for our faith. The greatest war that we are in right now is against the spirit of complacency. So many of us are lazy in our approach to growth in the Kingdom of God. In other words, we live our lives trapped in cycles of rejection, fear, anger, bitterness, self-hatred, and addiction, and we agree with the lie that this is our portion: "This is just the way things are." We deny the true power of the Gospel, and rather than stand and fight, we run toward comfort—food, sleep, pornography, entertainment—anything to numb us and take the edge off the pain without requiring us to exert ourselves. Although it is true that we receive salvation freely, we have to fight to gain breakthroughs and take ground in the Kingdom.

EPHESIANS 6

We are going to look at what Paul has to say about warfare and praying in the Spirit in his letter to the Ephesians. This is probably the most famous passage on spiritual warfare in the New Testament, but there are many other portions of Scripture where the subject of warfare is addressed.

> *For though we walk in the flesh, we do not war according to the flesh. For the weapons of our warfare are not carnal but mighty in God for pulling down strongholds* (2 Corinthians 10:3-4).

> *This charge I commit to you, son Timothy, according to the prophecies previously made concerning you, that by them you may wage the good warfare* (1 Timothy 1:18).

> *Fight the good fight of faith, lay hold on eternal life, to which you were also called and have confessed the good confession in the presence of many witnesses* (1 Timothy 6:12).

> *You therefore must endure hardship as a good soldier of Jesus Christ. No one engaged in warfare entangles*

himself with the affairs of this life, that he may please him who enlisted him as a soldier (2 Timothy 2:3-4).

I have fought the good fight of faith, I have finished the race, I have kept the faith (2 Timothy 4:7).

I found it necessary to write to you exhorting you to contend earnestly for the faith which was once for all delivered to the saints (Jude 3b).

Clearly the paradigm of warfare was foundational in the early Church. The apostles understood that the faith they were preaching could only be realized through arduous striving and contending. Consequently, they taught the first believers to expect and prepare for battle.

Paul's discussion of warfare in Ephesians 6 is prefaced by three chapters where he discusses the mystery of our union with Christ and three chapters where he teaches believers how to practically navigate life and relationships as those who are called to walk in the Spirit. His teaching on the armor of God concludes these discussions. Paul opens with this charge: *"Finally, my brethren, be strong in the Lord and in the power of His might"* (Eph. 6:10). Here we see that the call to warfare is the call to receive and live in the might of God. Paul tells the believers not to fight in their own strength with their own resources, but to put on Christ and His power. This is the foundational revelation to standing in the full armor of God and seeing victory in the arena of spiritual warfare; we have to consciously, deliberately put on Christ and receive His might, His life, His power.

It is often easy for us to pride ourselves on our own resources, but the Gospel demands that we constantly live in the reality of exchanging our strength for God's strength. *Praying in the Spirit is one of the most practical ways that we can lay down our own strength and be filled with divine provision.* In numerous epistles,

Paul called the churches to put off the old person and put on the new person—to put on Christ (see Rom. 14; Eph. 5; Col. 2). We must understand that we are in a spiritual battle and we must be spiritually equipped to stand and fight. We must cast off confidence in our own abilities, understanding, and resources, and cast ourselves on God for the reception of His life. The main pursuit of our lives must be the exchanging of our might for God's might, the transference of our abilities for God's abilities. When we pray in tongues, we are cultivating the connection between our spirits and the Spirit of Christ; we are experiencing the reality of union with God by the Holy Spirit.

It is when we try to live and fight solely on a horizontal plane that we end up getting pummeled. We must learn how to fight and train and condition ourselves in the Spirit. Galatians 5:16 says that if we walk in the Spirit, we will not fulfill the lusts of the flesh. When we fight in our own strength on a horizontal plane, then we never break through into the power of the Spirit that subdues the flesh and binds the enemy. We cannot kill the flesh with the flesh; power and victory only come from breakthrough in the Spirit. No amount of resolve or willpower can take the place of the Holy Spirit. Many in the Church are battling addictions, rejection, shame, guilt, and discouragement, and yet they do not look beyond their own resources for help to fight.

I want to clearly state that if you will begin to pray in the Spirit for extended periods of time, you will see the power of the enemy broken in your life, you will find your resolve divinely strengthened, and you will see your appetites alter and the desire for holiness increase. Break through into your spirit and live from there because if you don't you will be in trouble.

The weapons of our warfare are not carnal. We are not fighting a fleshly battle on a horizontal plane. This is a spiritual war!

Though we are in the flesh, we are called to be people who do not walk that way and do not think that way.

God wants to train us to fight and nothing prepares us for battle like the presence of an adversary. As we noted in the previous chapter, before David faced Goliath, he was a shepherd in Bethlehem who had to defend his flock against lions and bears. When no one was paying attention, David spent his time worshiping God and fighting the battles in front of him. He conquered the lion, the bear, the rejection and accusations of his family, and his own fears. Then, when Goliath appeared and all the warriors of Israel were overwhelmed, David stood with supernatural boldness and might in his spirit.

In the same way that Paul commanded Timothy to be ready in season and out of season (see 2 Tim. 4:2), so we must begin to develop spirits that are charged when we are in a manifestation season and charged when we are in a hidden season. If we can stay steady through every season, then we can be trusted with the greater authority that the Lord is releasing in this last generation. *Developing a history of speaking in tongues for extended periods of time is one of the primary ways that the Lord will train His army in these last days.*

It is important to remember this call to engage the divine strength of God as you begin to study the armor of God. Let's look at the rest of the passage:

> *Finally, my brethren, be strong in the Lord and in the power of His might. Put on the whole armor of God, that you may be able to stand against the wiles of the devil. For we do not wrestle against flesh and blood, but against principalities, against powers, against the rulers of the darkness of this age, against spiritual hosts of wickedness in the heavenly places. Therefore take*

up the whole armor of God, that you may be able to withstand in the evil day, and having done all, to stand.

Stand therefore, having girded your waist with truth, having put on the breastplate of righteousness, and having shod your feet with the preparation of the gospel of peace; above all, taking the shield of faith with which you will be able to quench all the fiery darts of the wicked one. And take the helmet of salvation, and the sword of the Spirit, which is the word of God; praying always with all prayer and supplication in the Spirit, being watchful to this end with all perseverance and supplication for all the saints (Ephesians 6:10-18).

After telling us that if we try to fight in our own strength we will be destroyed, Paul instructs us to put on the whole armor of God. It is important to note phrases such as *put on, take up,* and *stand.* Through these phrases Paul continually reminds us to put off our old person and to put on the new person, to put on Christ and walk in Him and who we are in Him and who He is in us. Jesus tells us in John 15 that we as branches are called to abide in the vine, for apart from Him we can do nothing. This is the same reality that Paul touches when he tells us to be strong in the power of His might. It is through the supply of the vine that the branches bear fruit. The source of fruitfulness in our life is abiding. This is the place of safety and authority.

The key reason that Paul calls us to put on Christ is for the purpose of standing against the wiles of the devil. As I have repeatedly emphasized, we are in a spiritual battle, and we must live in our spiritual identity to fight. A good friend recently told me, "What we fail to realize is that we have an enemy." As simple as it sounds, this is profoundly true. From the day that you and

I said yes to Jesus, we became the targets of the devil and all his demons. Satan hates us, and his occupation is to completely destroy the dream of God for each and every one of our lives. He wants to steal, kill, destroy, and devour us completely.

This is why it is imperative that we learn how to practically engage the life of God within us. Paul tells us that we must put on our armor—we must put on Christ—so that we can stand. Standing does not mean floating over every obstacle with no struggle and with complete victory, but it does mean determining in our hearts to walk in the fullness of God. When our hearts are set in this way and we fall, we are able to quickly rise and continue on. When we stand, we take ground in the Kingdom. This is the posture that equips us to resist every allurement and scheme of the devil.

I believe that the Lord is raising up a Joshua generation with a new spirit upon them—one that is not intimidated by the giants and has the courage to go to battle against anything in the name of Jesus. This generation will stop defining the normal Christian life as primarily defensive; they will move in to the offensive. Sometimes I think that in the spirit my life must look like a bad action movie—I am running around while bombs are raining down on me, and I don't have any thought beyond dodging the attacks. But it doesn't have to look like this. There is an invitation to stand in the might of God, put on the whole armor of God, and look beyond the battle with a spirit of faith. I want to be a part of the generation that takes ground with every step.

In verse 12, Paul tells us that we do not wrestle against flesh and blood. Our battlefield is in heavenly places where we contend against principalities, powers, and rulers. Are we connected with the reality that the battlefront in our lives is found in the supernatural realm? This is the same reality that we find in Daniel 10, where we get a rare glimpse into the supernatural battle raging in the heavens. As an old man, Daniel takes up the spiritual weapons of prayer, fasting, and the Word of God. He fasts for 21 days on behalf of the exiled nation of Israel, and at the end of his fast, a mighty angel appears and tells him that as he was praying, war was breaking out in the spirit realm.

> *Then he said to me, "Do not fear, Daniel, for from the first day that you set your heart to understand, and to humble yourself before your God, your words were heard; and I have come because of your words. But the prince of the kingdom of Persia withstood me twenty-one days; and behold, Michael, one of the chief princes, came to help me, for I had been left alone there with the kings of Persia"* (Daniel 10:12-13).

Here we see the direct relationship between our prayer and fasting and the battles being fought over the destinies of individuals and nations. We also see how different the weapons of the Spirit are from natural weapons. God's weapons are humility, weakness, gentleness, prayer, fasting, giving, and speaking in tongues. Through these unlikely tools God brings the powers of this age to nothing.

"Therefore take up the whole armor of God, that you may be able to withstand in the evil day, and having done all, to stand" (Eph. 6:13). As we continue looking at this passage, we see that Paul highlights the escalation of warfare at the end of the age. The phrase *the evil day* refers to a specific time in human history: the final three and a half years preceding the second coming of Christ, also known as the Great Tribulation, Jacob's Trouble, or the time of trouble. This is when the antichrist, possessed by satan himself, will unleash violence throughout the Earth for the purpose of annihilating Jews and those who stand with them—including the Church. In Revelation 12, as in Daniel 10, we get to see what this

battle will look like from a heavenly perspective as the prayers of the saints tip the balance against satan and he is cast from Heaven to Earth. Although his rage is great, there is supernatural strength and protection released for the people of God:

> *Now when the dragon saw that he had been cast to the earth, he persecuted the woman who gave birth to the male Child. But the woman was given two wings of a great eagle, that she might fly into the wilderness to her place, where she is nourished for a time and times and half a time, from the presence of the serpent. So the serpent spewed water out of his mouth like a flood after the woman, that he might cause her to be carried away by the flood. But the earth helped the woman, and the earth opened its mouth and swallowed up the flood which the dragon had spewed out of his mouth. And the dragon was enraged with the woman, and he went to make war with the rest of her offspring, who keep the commandments of God and have the testimony of Jesus Christ* (Revelation 12:13-17).

With such realities in mind, it is no wonder that Paul again exhorts us to stand. We have need of great strength, courage, and perseverance if we are to stay steady in the midst of such persecution and warfare! *"Stand therefore"*—above all this is our charge. We must stand and remain standing, abiding in Christ and receiving the strength that He imparts. Paul describes this strength using the metaphors of armor. Each piece of armor represents a different aspect of the life of God that is available to us. We have received His truth, His righteousness, His peace, His faith, and His salvation—but we won't experience what we have received unless we engage the life of God within. Christ *is* our armor; He is the way, the truth, and the life, and we must connect with His Spirit living inside us in order to be fully equipped for battle.

Instead of spending time examining each piece of armor, I want to focus on the two offensive weapons Paul mentions at the end of the passage. I do want to briefly highlight the shield of faith, though. Paul particularly emphasizes this piece of armor when he writes, *"above all, taking the shield of faith with which you will be able to quench all the fiery darts of the wicked one"* (Eph. 6:16). The fiery darts that the shield of faith protects us from are not metaphorical; the enemy really does release arrows of accusation, confusion, despair, fear, lust, and so forth, which are meant to wound and paralyze us. I have learned to recognize the symptoms of these missiles in my own life: when a fiery dart comes against me, my thoughts are chaotic and confused, and my emotions are charged with intense, negative feelings that have little to do with reality. Sometimes these feelings will last for only minutes or hours and sometimes for days. But Paul lets us know that we have a shield that can prevent many of these attacks from seriously affecting us.

When we pray in the spirit, we are building up our defense system—we are constructing a force field around ourselves in the spirit. Proverbs says, *"Whoever has no rule over his own spirit is like a city broken down, without walls"* (Prov. 25:28). In other words, our ability to strengthen our spirits and walk in faith can determine how vulnerable we are to the attacks of the enemy. We can construct walls around our lives in the spirit that prevent many of the enemy's missiles from reaching us. The fiery darts of the enemy are just a reality of life in this age, but I believe that a significant number of the assignments that come against us can be aborted and destroyed if we will take the time to build a force field in the spirit. We will not know on this side of eternity how many attacks we avoided by engaging the life of God within and building up our spirits, but I believe we can substantially decrease the demonic activity in our lives. And even if the attack is not prevented, we have the ability to walk through the storm with the peace of God. We will understand that we are not alone, and we will be able to pull on the life and strength of God in the midst of the battle.

The first five elements of the armor of God (truth, righteousness, peace, faith, salvation) are defensive in nature, and each one of these is vital to the life of the believer. However, God has also given us two offensive weapons: the Word of God and praying in the Spirit. I want to look at these two weapons because they are more than nice options; these are the two stones the Lord has given us to defeat the kingdom of darkness.

> *And take...the sword of the Spirit, which is the word of God; praying always with all prayer and supplication in the Spirit, being watchful to this end with all perseverance and supplication for all the saints* (Ephesians 6:17-18).

The most powerful force in the earth is the Word of God. Through the spoken word the heavens and Earth were created. The Scriptures say God's Word is living and active, sharper than any two-edged sword; it cuts, pierces, divides, and exposes. The Word of God has creative power, and when it is spoken by prepared vessels, it releases prophetic realities on Earth. In Psalm 149 we find a picture of the end-time Church operating in its identity as the army of God. It says that the high praises of God are in the mouths of the saints and a two-edged sword is in their hands. Today we are witnessing a worship and prayer movement arise all over the Earth; as the Word of God is released through song and prayer, the powers of darkness will be driven back. Faith is imparted through the spoken Word of God. Even now the Lord is training an army that knows how to sit before His Word and receive divine strength, faith, and revelation.

In Second Chronicles 20, Jerusalem is in a military crisis. King Jehoshaphat called Jerusalem to a fast, and during the fast, the Lord released a prophetic word promising the defeat of their enemies. In response, the king appointed singers to go out before the army, praising the Lord. As they sang, God ambushed and destroyed the enemy; every man died. This gives us amazing insight into the strategy of the Lord in warfare. Singing and declaring the Word of God will break the power of every enemy. This is the same reality that Daniel operated in during his fast recorded in Daniel 10. The angel that appeared to him on the twenty-first day of the fast told him that his prayers had released the power necessary to break through the demonic principality over Persia.

The second offensive weapon Paul lists immediately after the sword of the spirit is praying in the Spirit: *"praying always with all prayer and supplication in the Spirit, being watchful to this end with all perseverance and supplication for all the saints."* One of the main weapons that the Lord has given the Church is praying in the Spirit. This is not limited to tongues, but speaking in tongues is one of the most powerful and effective ways to pray in the Spirit. The power of praying in tongues is that we begin to see and hear and perceive what is going on in the Spirit. Paul says that we should always pray in the Spirit in order to remain *watchful;* when we speak in tongues, the strategies of Heaven and hell are revealed. Praying in the Spirit enables us to stand in watchfulness. It is like shining a light into the darkness and beginning to see what is in the unseen. As we pray in tongues for extended periods of time, we receive insights into the plans of God and the schemes of the devil, and we are equipped with the Word of God to destroy those schemes. In 2 Corinthians 2:11, Paul says that we are not unaware of the enemy's schemes. We are forewarned by the Spirit and are given the necessary weapons to expose and destroy the fiery darts of the enemy.

One of my good friends had a dream several years ago related to the power of praying and singing in the Spirit as a weapon of warfare. Here she shares the dream in her own words:

> Many of us were in the prayer room, but we knew it to be a class room. We thought we were in high school, but then our leader welcomed us to kindergarten. He invited us to read Ephesians 6, so we all opened our Bibles and began reading.
>
> Meanwhile many black demons began to fill our classroom. We all were very intrigued. We stopped reading and felt like we needed to do something—to engage or speak to these demons. With authority, our leader told us to keep reading and not to be distracted by the demons. It seemed like years went by as we filled ourselves with the Word of God.
>
> Then our leader said "The time has come to sing." We all rose to our feet and began to sing in the Spirit. As we sang we began to ascend up these stairs. Before we knew it, we were on the top of a high tower in the city. Our voices continued to make melody to the Lord—high praises were coming forth—and strongholds over entire cities were being taken down. Witches and principalities were coming against us, but as we sang, judgment was executed upon everything that exalted itself above Him. I remember the tangible might of God I felt exude from me as I sang and the joy I experienced as our eyes were upon Him.

As stated earlier in Chapter 6, speaking in tongues is also the most effective means of training ourselves to wield the sword of the Spirit with power. This sword is our most powerful weapon, but it will do us no good if we are not able to carry it with authority.

Two people can pray the same prayer, word for word, yet when one of them prays, it seems that angels and demons move in the room. This is due to the issue of strength of spirit. People who shake the atmosphere and send darkness fleeing when they proclaim the Word of God have spent time edifying and strengthening themselves so that they wield the sword of the Spirit effectively. People who have not built up their spirit may speak the same words and pray the same prayers, but the proclamations fall to the ground with no life or power in them. What was meant to be a sword is more like a butter knife in their hands. We must decide today to take up the weapons we have been given and train our spirits through abiding in the Word and speaking in tongues so that we can push back darkness in our lives and the lives of others.

In our discipleship of the next generation, we must begin to teach the daily discipline of praying for extended, undistracted periods of time in tongues. The overflow of these times of prayer will be the release of the Word of God in power through song and proclamation. I find that when I daily put my hand to the plow and press against my circumstances, I receive fresh releases of the presence of God within me. This equips me to stand against the wiles of the devil and grow in my awareness of the battle that is going on around me. I believe it opens up the door for a thousand other evils when we have weak spirits that cannot ward off the demonic attacks the enemy throws our way. So many Christians do not know how to break the power of oppression over their own spirits. Instead of taking up the weapons we have been given, we sit around and complain about the resistance that we are facing spiritually. We are so quick to say, "It's just one of those seasons," and fall into the familiar, comfortable trap of self-pity. It is time for believers to rise up, shut the door against defeat and pity, set their eyes on the throne, and bless the Lord with their spirits until the life of God that is within them puts the enemy to flight.

Chapter 8

THE KEY TO
TRANSFORMATION

I have spent several chapters now discussing the many benefits of praying in the Spirit. This gift escorts us into the realm of revelation and unlocks the mysteries of God; it strengthens our spirits, builds us up personally and corporately, and is a vital weapon in the arena of spiritual warfare. However, more than all of these, the greatest benefit that I have experienced from praying in the Spirit for extended periods of time is the transformation it has produced in my own heart and life. The Holy Spirit's first name is Holy, and His primary job is to transform us into the image of Christ. So often the charismatic church loses sight of this truth. Though we may grow in spiritual gifts, our inward lives deteriorate more and more. However, I have found that as I begin to deliberately engage the Holy Spirit through praying in tongues, even in my most difficult seasons, He rises up within my inner person, changing and transforming me.

Let me give you an example: I travel quite a bit, speaking at various churches and conferences nationally and internationally.

Often after long stretches of travelling or seasons of busyness, all I want to do is go home, lock my door, eat everything in the house, then sit on the couch and watch sports on the television for a week or two. Sometimes I do it, and I find measures of rest, but the ultimate rest I am looking for isn't found on a couch or in front of a television. The rest and refreshing that I'm looking for is found in sitting before the Lord and communing with Him through extended times of praying in tongues. Isaiah 28 states this:

> *For with stammering lips and another tongue He will speak to this people, to whom He said, "This is the rest with which you may cause the weary to rest," and, "This is the refreshing"...* (Isaiah 28:11-12).

I have learned that when I am tired and battling fleshly desires, if I begin to pray in the Spirit and press into God then my fatigue will gradually leave and my heart will rise above the desires of the flesh and reconnect with the desires of the Spirit. Sometimes it takes a while for my emotions and my body to switch gears. There have been instances when I have begun to pray in the Spirit and then have made difficult decisions to spend my time in a godly way, even though I would really rather be lazing around, but when I engage the life of the Holy Spirit through tongues, eventually my soul and my body are brought into alignment with God.

SANCTIFICATION

The work of sanctification is one of the least talked about, written about, or discussed subjects when it comes to the Person and ministry of the Holy Spirit. But the truth is that He has come to make us like Him, and as we engage Him, His life and His holiness flow in us and through us. It is only through abiding in the vine that the life of the vine is released in the branches.

Praying in the Spirit is one of the means by which we abide in God and He conforms us to the image of His Son. It is a critical tool in the process of sanctification and an on-ramp into accelerated character transformation. Unfortunately, many of us have taken this gift and turned it into a badge, an empty sign of spirituality.

Why is it that so many Christians have received the baptism of the Spirit, and yet we look very little like Christ? Instead, we remain prisoners of bitterness, anger, jealousy, and lust. I believe this is because we do not understand that speaking in tongues is actually an escort into the Person of Jesus. It is not about checking a gift off a list—"Yes, I speak in tongues"—but it is about engaging and talking to a Person who wants to change us.

> *Now may the God of peace Himself sanctify you completely; and may your whole spirit, soul, and body be preserved blameless at the coming of our Lord Jesus Christ* (1 Thessalonians 5:23).

In First Thessalonians we see a description of God's ultimate goal for the life of every believer. Salvation includes more than our justification. Not only are we given right standing with God, but we are also set apart in order that we might be transformed into the image of Christ—body, soul, and spirit. This is sanctification; it is the process of driving out all sin and setting us apart to receive the holiness of God. One day we will be completely transformed and will stand before Him blameless. In the meantime, the Holy Spirit within us is laboring to produce the character of Christ in our lives.

When talking to the Corinthians in 2 Corinthians 6:16, Paul highlights the understanding that they are the temple of the Living God, and that God dwells in them. It's through this revelation that Paul exhorts them to come out from among all forms of sin and compromise. He calls the Church, in light of these glorious realities, to cleanse themselves *"from all filthiness of the flesh and spirit, perfecting holiness in the fear of God"* (2 Cor. 7:1). He is holy and He lives within us to make us a holy habitation for Jesus. We must begin to actively engage His life within us and we will witness the power of His life over all sin and compromise.

THE LAW OF THE SPIRIT

For the law of the Spirit of life in Christ Jesus has made me free from the law of sin and death (Romans 8:2).

We see in this passage that there are two contrasting laws. What is a law? In government, a law establishes consequences for various actions. If I speed while driving, I will receive a ticket and be required to pay a fine. Laws function similarly in the realm of science and physics. According to the law of gravity, if I jump from a cliff I will fall, not fly. Laws reveal the consequences connected to actions: if you do A, you will get B. The law of the Old Covenant is no different. It shows us that the consequence connected to sin is death. There is a problem with this law, though: it does not empower us to stop sinning and live righteously. And because we cannot stop sinning, this law imprisons us in life and seals us in death.

Under this law people's inability to follow God is fully exposed. The law is a mirror that shows us our wickedness and causes us to wrestle with the fact that we fall utterly short of God's standards of righteousness. It is more than a mirror, though; God gave us the law of the Old Covenant to reveal our need for a savior. The revelation of our sinfulness creates in our hearts the need and desire for a person to do what we cannot do on our own: to fulfill the righteous requirements of the law. Romans 3:19 says that the purpose of the law is to shut every mouth. In other words, the law exists to silence our attempts at justification. Galatians 3:24 says that the law is a tutor to bring us to Christ.

The good news is that God was not content to leave us in prison. Instead, He sent His Son to live under and fulfill the law, thereby breaking its dominion (see Gal. 4:1-7). Jesus came and joined hands with us when we were prisoners. He took on our likeness and He lived under the law without sin. Then, in the fullness of time, He redeemed us from the bondage of the law by paying the penalty of bloodshed it required, thereby destroying its power over us. Through the cross we have been conveyed into a new Kingdom with a higher law. The law of the Spirit is the reality that we are now able to transcend the old law and to live as God designed. Paul says, in essence, "You are under a new governmental system, and if you live according to this system, you will transcend that which used to hold you down. There is no more condemnation. There is no more bondage, no more slavery to sin, no more doing what you didn't want to do—you are liberated from that by Jesus."

WALKING IN THE SPIRIT = PRAYING IN THE SPIRIT

Paul restates the law of the Spirit in his letter to the Galatians.

> *I say then: Walk in the Spirit, and you shall not fulfill the lust of the flesh. For the flesh lusts against the Spirit, and the Spirit against the flesh; and these are contrary to one another, so that you do not do the things that you wish. But if you are led by the Spirit, you are not under the law* (Galatians 5:16-18).

This is the new law: if you walk in the Spirit, you will not fulfill the lust of the flesh. Paul is emphatic—he does not say maybe, he says that we *will not* fulfill the lusts of the flesh. In other words, if we walk in the Spirit, we will not view pornography, give into fits of rage, harbor bitterness and resentment, or say yes to a thousand other evils. We are truly in the midst of an internal war in which the flesh and the Spirit are absolutely contrary to one another. These two are always battling for dominance in our hearts, and if we are not submitting to one, we are automatically allowing the other to rule over us. Look at what the lust of the flesh produces in our lives:

> *Now the works of the flesh are evident, which are: adultery, fornication, uncleanness, lewdness, idolatry, sorcery, hatred, contentions, jealousies, outbursts of wrath, selfish ambitions, dissensions, heresies, envy, murders, drunkenness, revelries, and the like...* (Galatians 5:19-21).

In contrast, here is what the Spirit produces in us:

> *But the fruit of the Spirit is love, joy, peace, long-suffering, kindness, goodness, faithfulness, gentleness, self-control. Against such there is no law* (Galatians 5:22-23).

Many of us are guilty of becoming so familiar with this passage that it has ceased to mean much. We need to be reminded that this fruit is actually a by-product of a Person. God is love, joy, and peace, and we only experience these things in our lives when we are connected to Him.

> *Do not be deceived, God is not mocked; for whatever a man sows, that he will also reap. For he who sows to his flesh will of the flesh reap corruption, but he*

who sows to the Spirit will of the Spirit reap everlasting life (Galatians 6:7-8).

Here Paul articulates another law: the law of sowing and reaping. The language he uses to illustrate his point is taken from agriculture. When a farmer sows wheat, he will reap wheat. If he plants tomatoes he will not harvest apples, but tomatoes. The same is true when it comes to the things of the Spirit. Paul warns us not to falsely believe that we can follow after the lusts of our flesh and still reap the fruit of the Holy Spirit. We can fill ourselves with the things of the world, but if we do so, we will be emptied of the things of the Spirit. Our hearts will grow colder as we reject the love of God, we will be weighed down and unable to experience joy, and we will grow in anxiety and fear rather than peace.

What do these laws have to do with tongues? The answer lies in the commandment to walk in the Spirit. According to Paul, if we walk in the Spirit then we will fulfill the righteous requirement of the law and reap the fruit of the Spirit. I believe that praying in tongues is one of the most effective and practical ways to walk in the Spirit. *When we speak in tongues, we are engaging the Person who empowers us to live above the law of sin and death.* After praying in the Spirit for extended periods of time, we are strengthened in our ability to say no to the lusts of the flesh. We are actually activating the law of the Spirit in our lives as we commune with the Holy Spirit.

Praying in tongues is sowing to the Spirit; it is planting the things of the Spirit in the garden of our hearts, and if we keep sowing those seeds, we will eventually reap a harvest. We may not see the fruit right away—there are sowing seasons and reaping seasons in the spirit just as there are in the natural. This is why Paul tells us not to grow weary: *"And let us not grow weary while doing good, for in due season we shall reap if we do not lose heart"* (Gal. 6:9). We need to persevere in the sowing season and not grow weary in the midst of our labor. The fruit will come if we do not give up.

Chapter 9

RECEIVING AND SUSTAINING LIFE IN THE SPIRIT

In this chapter, I want to take a practical, nuts-and-bolts look at how to begin and then sustain a life of praying in the spirit, both individually and corporately. If you have never heard any teaching on the gift of tongues and are hungry to actually step out and receive your prayer language, then this chapter is for you. However, whether or not you have personally received the gift of tongues, this chapter contains insight and revelation about releasing tongues and pastorally overseeing the use of tongues in the community—revelation that will hopefully serve and equip every reader. There are several critical things that I believe will help you as you seek to operate in this gift and pastor it in others: releasing and receiving the baptism of the Spirit, manifestations, prep rooms, and the need to cultivate a culture of honor and love.

RECEIVING THE BAPTISM OF THE SPIRIT

If a son asks for bread from any father among you,
will he give him a stone? Or if he asks for a fish, will

he give him a serpent instead of a fish? Or if he asks
for an egg, will he offer him a scorpion? If you then,
being evil, know how to give good gifts to your chil-
dren, how much more will your heavenly Father give
the Holy Spirit to those who ask Him (Luke 11:11-13).

In this passage Jesus declares that our Father in Heaven is infinitely more generous, tender, glad, and good than any earthly father. He loves to give good gifts to His children; He loves to fill His sons and daughters with the Holy Spirit, not just once or twice, but regularly and frequently. Whenever I lead anyone in receiving the baptism of the Holy Spirit, I begin with this truth. Many of us experience unnecessary pain in our pursuit of the gift of tongues because our hearts are not grounded in the love of the Father. Our fear and insecurity actually shut down our capacity to receive, and then we think that God must not want us to have this gift! However, in 15 years of ministry, I have yet to meet a believer whom God did not want to baptize with His Spirit. He is a good Father and loves to release His gifts to those who are hungry for them.

Everything in the Kingdom of God is accessed by faith, and so it is with receiving the personal gift of tongues. God stirs our hearts, but we must respond and step out in faith to receive from Him. Peter could not walk on the water while he was in the boat; he had to move his body and climb out of the boat in order to experience the power of walking on water. Prophetic ministry is an excellent example of this principle. Often, when we are praying for people and asking the Lord to speak to them, a faint impression, image, or word will come to mind. It is not overwhelming; the audible voice of God does not knock us over. Instead, He releases these gentle impressions and waits to see if we will step out and share, in faith, what we are hearing. More times than not, when we share what He has given, a greater flow of revelation is released. Additional words and pictures come, and the individual receiving ministry is deeply touched and blessed.

God has a part, and we have a part; this truth is clearly manifested when it comes to receiving the baptism of the Spirit. God will do His part by causing His presence to gently and subtly well up within us, but we must do ours by opening our hearts and speaking what comes out in faith. This can be a stumbling block for many people. Some of us are so determined to only experience the real things of God (and so afraid of falling prey to something that is fake or hyped or demonic), that we stand with our jaws clenched and wait for God to come down, pry open our mouths, and forcibly move our tongues. I appreciate the desire for something real, but we do not need to be afraid of responding in faith when we feel the presence of the Holy Spirit rising up within us. This is God's way of letting us know that He is ready to release the gift of tongues if we will just say yes and begin to pray. In fact, I have found that most individuals only have to ask in faith and simplicity; nine times out of ten, when we do this and then open our mouths, the river is released and flows effortlessly from within us.

Although for many the baptism of the Spirit is experienced as easily as I have described, there are a few common roadblocks to receiving our prayer language that I would like to address. The first roadblock is fear and anxiety. When I minister to individuals who want to receive their prayer language, I begin by telling them to chill out. There is nothing we can do to earn this gift; striving and performing will not get us anywhere. I like to use the analogy of a child on Christmas morning. How many of us, when we were little, woke up on Christmas morning and looked for ways to earn our presents? Did we work our way down a list of chores so that we could open the packages under the tree? No, children innately understand how to receive gifts with confidence.

And God wants His children to have the same confidence in Him. It is not uncommon to see individuals who are anxious or overwhelmed during a ministry time. They are praying up a storm, begging and pleading and bargaining and laboring in their efforts to receive their prayer language because they don't believe this gift is really for them. When I see people struggling in this way, I encourage them to do a few things: open their hearts, lift their heads, and quietly say, "I receive." I even encourage them to take deep breaths and just wait before the Lord. The truth is that God wants to give us the Holy Spirit more than we want it, so we can rest in His goodness and generosity.

The second roadblock is related to judgment. If individuals are consistently facing resistance while trying to receive their prayer language, I will encourage them to ask the Lord to highlight any areas of sin He would like to address. If we have not repented of sin and entered into agreement with God in significant areas of our lives, this can block the activity of the Holy Spirit. Sometimes the issue is not our sin; sometimes we face resistance because our parents or grandparents rejected the move of the Holy Spirit.[1] If a relative denounced the gift of tongues, this can create a ceiling in the spirit over the next generation; these are called generational curses. We can actually reap judgments that are released through generational lines. The good news is that God delights in mercy and the blood of Jesus is more powerful than the blood that runs in our families.

I ministered to one young man whose grandfather was firmly convinced that the gift of tongues was of the devil. I encouraged him to forgive and bless his grandfather, to plead the blood of Jesus over his family line, and then to make these simple declarations: "I love You, Holy Spirit" and "I want all that You have for me, Holy Spirit." As he began to do this, the floodgates opened and his new prayer language came rushing out.

The last roadblock that I commonly encounter when leading people in receiving the baptism of the Spirit is the issue of humility. Our minds can be the greatest barrier when it comes to entering the Kingdom with faith like a child. Many people can quench the release of this gift in their lives without realizing it. They feel the Spirit rising up within them, a phrase is on the tip of their tongues, and then their minds object: *That doesn't make sense. You're making that up. You will sound ridiculous if you pray that phrase.* Once we say yes to those thoughts, the Holy Spirit will not force Himself past our objections.

However, I have found that it often helps to remind ourselves that the wisdom of God is foolishness to people (see 1 Cor. 1:20-31). His ways are not our ways, and He doesn't mind if we sound ridiculous; if we are hungry enough, we will eventually stop caring about our reputations. Some people find it helpful to repeat phrases after the person praying for them in order to overcome the initial barriers in their minds. Once their mouth is moving, they easily transition into praying in the Spirit. It is also important to remember that we are not trying to produce a specific sound. We must not judge and evaluate our prayer languages or compare them to the languages of those around us.

PRAYER TO RECEIVE TONGUES

If you would like to receive your prayer language, here is a simple prayer that you can pray:

> *Father, I ask in the name of Jesus that You would fill me with Holy Spirit from the top of my head to the soles of my feet. I want to speak in tongues, I want to prophesy, I want to receive visitations and encounters—I want all that You have for me. Thank You for the good gifts that You give.*

After praying and simply asking for the Holy Spirit, all you have to do is quietly wait. The gift of tongues might explode out of your spirit quickly and powerfully, or you might need to spend some time sitting in the presence of God. If you are responding to an altar call during a ministry time, you will probably need to soak in the anointed atmosphere for a while and allow God to tenderize your heart. Most of us need a little encouragement to go to that vulnerable place where our defenses are lowered and we are actually able to receive. After 15 years of ministry, I have found that I can usually tell when people stop striving and start receiving. When I see this transition, I will approach them and tell them to just start speaking out what God is giving.

TOOLS AND INSIGHTS FOR THE JOURNEY

In the second chapter we looked at the different pictures of the Holy Spirit found in Scripture. What many believers discover when they receive their prayer language, however, is that these are not just pictures—they are experiences that are available to us. There are many manifestations of the Spirit: the fire of His presence can produce tears, a tenderizing of our hearts and physical sensations of heat; His light and glory are often experienced as a weighty presence, and some find it difficult to stand or move when they encounter this manifestation; the river of the Spirit brings deep refreshing and life to our souls; the wine of the Spirit releases joy and laughter (see Acts 2:4-13); the wind of the Holy Spirit is often an indication of angelic activity, and many people receive physical healing when they encounter this particular manifestation. This is not an exhaustive list, but these are some of the encounters that are available to those who have been baptized in the Spirit.

Some believers—and even some denominations—place a lot of emphasis on these manifestations of the Spirit. It can be easy for us to lose sight of the Person we are communing with if we are constantly preoccupied with the effects of His presence. Therefore, it is important to remember that the ultimate purpose of praying in the Spirit is not experiencing physical manifestations; it is communing with the One whom we love. However, the truth is that God designed humanity to enjoy relationship with Him. God is a God of pleasure, and we are meant to experience pleasure as we connect with Him.

Look at what Paul writes to the Ephesians: *"Do not get drunk on wine, which leads to debauchery. Instead, be filled with the Spirit"* (Eph. 5:18 NIV). The apostle Paul actually declares that being filled with the Holy Spirit is a superior pleasure in comparison to being drunk in the natural. In Song of Solomon the maiden says that God's love is better than wine (see Song of Sol. 1:2b). Nothing is more powerful or more pleasurable than when God, through the gift of tongues and through His Word, touches the human spirit. Do we realize what we have been given?

> *In Your presence is fullness of joy; at Your right hand are pleasures forevermore* (Psalm 16:11b).

> *They are abundantly satisfied with the fullness of Your house, and You give them drink from the river of Your pleasures* (Psalm 36:8).

We don't have to repent of our desire for pleasure. The religious spirit wants us to believe that this desire is sinful, but the truth is that it is part of our created design. Everyone will be drunk on something—that is not the issue. The real issue is this: *What will fill us? What will intoxicate us?* When someone is drunk, we say they are "under the influence." Whose influence are we under? What controls our passions, our emotions, and our desires? We are made to be filled with God, and if we neglect this reality, we will end up spiritually bored and vulnerable to temptation, sin, and darkness.

I have found that one of the primary ways of accessing the realm of spiritual pleasure is through praying and singing in the Spirit. In Ephesians 5, after Paul tells believers to be filled with the Holy Spirit, he then goes on to tell them how to be filled: singing in the Spirit is the key to receiving increasing measures of the Spirit (see Eph. 5:19). Paul states this clearly in his letter to the Corinthians, at the end of chapter 14:

> *What is the conclusion then? I will pray with the spirit, and I will also pray with the understanding. I will sing with the spirit, and I will also sing with the understanding* (1 Corinthians 14:15).

Why does Paul differentiate between speaking and singing in tongues? I believe that when we sing in the Spirit, we experience deeper realities in God. Our hearts open in a unique way through music, and a different part of our souls is touched and moved by song. When we sing, the Word of God penetrates our hearts at deeper levels. This is how God designed us, and He desires to satisfy every part of our being with His presence. I don't usually worry about determining when I should pray versus when I should sing; I practice both interchangeably and follow the gentle leading of the Holy Spirit. As long as we are hungry for encounter and sensitive to His presence, He will lead us where we need to go.

I love the pleasures of God, but I don't base my faith on them. At the end of the day, our walk with the Lord is not about how we feel, and neither is our practice of spiritual disciplines. Throughout this book I have talked about the need for perseverance when it comes to speaking in tongues. This is because it is easy to hide behind the excuse that we don't feel the Spirit.

Many individuals wait until they are falling over at an altar call before they speak in tongues, and then they wonder why they don't see more consistent fruit in their lives. The truth is that if I only spoke in tongues when I felt overpowered by the presence of God, I would hardly ever do it. I almost never feel like praying in the Spirit initially, but I have settled it in my heart that this is an issue of obedience, strength, and resolve, and so I press through the initial resistance.

The author of Hebrews says that we must labor to enter into rest (see Heb. 4:11). There is a place of rest for our spirits where God releases supernatural grace and allows us to experience the pleasures of His presence; in that place of rest, what was difficult before suddenly becomes effortless and refreshing. However, in order to enter that place of rest, we must labor by saying no to distractions, committing our hearts even when we don't feel like it, and pressing in until we get breakthrough.

The good news is that, in the midst of the season of laboring, there is a powerful reality that will sustain us: God is on His throne, Jesus is seated at His right hand, and we have been given access into that holy place. And when we begin to pray in the Spirit, it does not matter how we feel; the truth is that we are priests who are called to awaken our spirits and bless the Lord, and we stand in heavenly places by faith and praise God. We don't enter into Heaven based on what we feel, our track record, our successes, or our failures. We enter in through the blood of the spotless Lamb, and we stand on the sea of glass described in Revelation 4, and we bless the Lord with our mouths; we thank and praise Him, we glorify Him with our spirits, and we minister to His heart. This is the reality that we enter into every time we pray in the Spirit.

Where and when can we engage in tongues? I recommend setting aside 20 to 30 minutes every day to intentionally pray in the Spirit. This is just the beginning, though. We can commune with the Holy Spirit in the car, at work, at school, at home, while we're running errands, in a worship service—the reality of fellowshipping with the Holy Spirit is available to us constantly. I have a deep desire to see believers transform their cars into chambers of encounter during their morning and evening commutes. So often we use those hours on the road to listen to talk shows, sports radio, or even good Christian songs, when we could be fellowshipping with God and touching the life of Heaven.

What does this look like practically? If you are at school, take the few minutes of chaos before class starts and quiet your soul, fix your eyes on the throne room of Revelation 4, and pray quietly under your breath. If you are at work, take several two-minute breaks throughout the day and meditate on Colossians 1:27—Christ in you—as you gently engage in tongues.

Wherever we are, when we begin to pray in the Spirit, these are our focal points: God on the throne and God in our spirit, God eternal and God internal. The more we find these moments of communion and fellowship throughout the day, the more we will connect with the realities of Heaven. In First Thessalonians 5:17 we are exhorted to pray without ceasing. Speaking in tongues is a powerful way to cultivate unceasing prayer in our lives, turn our thoughts into prayers, and direct our internal thoughts and conversations to God.

Do not be discouraged if you struggle to stay focused. Your mind will want to run everywhere because you are human, and that is what human minds do. Whenever you catch yourself wandering off, just bring your focus back to God. This will get easier over time, and you will actually train your mind to meditate on and be preoccupied with the things of the Spirit. This is called renewing your mind.

I have found that when I pray in the spirit for extended periods of time (20 minutes or more), the first 15 minutes or so of prayer I spend battling distractions and fighting to connect with the Holy Spirit. At around the 20-minute mark, however, it is as if the atmosphere around me clears; suddenly my mind is sharp and my gaze is locked on God, and I feel the Spirit rise up within me and begin to pray. I sense a shift in the spiritual atmosphere around me when I press into God through praying in the Spirit. I also believe that there is an increase in angelic ministry.

After those first 20 minutes of struggle, prayers and phrases begin to arise spontaneously from my spirit. "God, I bless You. There is none like You. You are beautiful, You are glorious, You are holy." This is when I enter into the revelatory realm of worship, prayer, and prophetic insight. The Word of God comes to life inside of me, and I rise above the storm clouds of my circumstances. This is the ladder that we discussed in Chapter 7—the ladder where angels are ascending and descending as we become the very house of God.

Many of us have read the verse that says when we pray in tongues, our minds are unfruitful (see 1 Cor. 14:14). It is true that speaking in tongues bypasses our natural reason; we don't know what we are praying, and so our minds cannot process what is happening. However, I have found that though my understanding is not immediately benefitted, over time I am escorted into deeper realms of revelation, knowledge, and faith. I have heard countless similar testimonies over my years of teaching on this subject, so be encouraged. If you stay with it, you will go somewhere in the Spirit. You really will experience breakthrough and enter into heavenly realities.

PREP ROOMS

For the last five years I have been leading prep rooms at IHOP. The term "prep rooms" refers to the activity of praying in the Spirit for the purpose of preparing ourselves for intercession. Thirty to 45 minutes before a corporate intercession meeting, we will gather a small group of people together in a room and begin to speak in tongues in order to clear our minds, align our souls, and break through to the heart of Jesus. The power of intercession lies in our faith and confidence that God hears us and that we are praying according to His will.

> *Now this is the confidence that we have in Him, that if we ask anything according to His will, He hears us. And if we know that He hears us, whatever we ask, we know that we have the petitions that we have asked of Him* (1 John 5:14-15).

As we pray in tongues for extended periods of time, we are filled with the knowledge of His will, and we gain confidence and faith in our prayers. And when we do not know what to pray, the Holy Spirit prays through us in alignment with the will of God as we speak in tongues (see Rom. 8:26).

We want to receive the prayers and faith of God and move in unity with Him. When we spend time praying in the Spirit, we engage in intercession with greater faith and we release the prayers of Heaven on Earth. We also keep one another accountable; most of us find that we pray in the Spirit more often when we set aside times to do it together.

If you want to establish prep rooms of your own, it is critical to assemble a group of like-minded believers who are unified in their desire to press into God through tongues. However, even when the group is united in desire, it can be difficult to help people with different backgrounds and personalities successfully engage in prayer simultaneously. When leading a prep room, I ask everyone to pray in tongues at 50 percent of their natural volume and intensity. I find that this encourages the quiet people to step up and the loud people to step down so that the entire room can go somewhere together. In this environment, everyone feels free to join in, and no one person hijacks the meeting.

Here is one final note: keep the group focused on praying in the Spirit. A prep room is not the place to preach, share dreams and visions, or prophesy over one another. It is not even the place to pray extensively in English. In my experience, groups will easily drift off course and begin to engage in tongues less and less over time unless there is a leader present who is reminding the group of its vision and purpose.

CREATING A CULTURE OF LOVE AND HONOR

The apostle Paul was the greatest advocate for the use of spiritual gifts. In his letter to the Corinthians, he affirmed the glory and power of speaking in tongues and encouraged every believer to pursue all the gifts of the Spirit wholeheartedly. But that was not all that Paul had to say on the subject. In the midst of his discussion of the gifts and how they ought to operate in the Body of Christ, Paul included a lengthy exhortation on what he called the more excellent way: love. First Corinthians 13 is one of the best-known chapters in the Bible, yet few people realize that these verses about the nature of love were written to help the church at Corinth operate in the gifts, and specifically the gift of tongues, in corporate settings.

Paul had a radical revelation of the love of Christ. In his epistle to the Philippians, he described the lengths that Jesus went to in order to save and redeem us, all for the sake of love:

> *Let this mind be in you which was also in Christ Jesus, who, being in the form of God, did not consider it robbery to be equal with God, but made Himself of no reputation, taking the form of a bondservant, and coming in the likeness of men* (Philippians 2:5-7).

In other words, although it was within His rights to retain equality with God, Jesus voluntarily and joyfully surrendered that equality and became a servant in order to raise up the lowly ones. This is the standard and the model for believers; we are called to love as we have been loved. And according to Paul, love does not seek its own (see 1 Cor. 13:5). Instead, it always seeks to honor, serve, edify, and bless others.

How does this apply to the gift of tongues? The answer is simple: corporate settings are not the place for the full and free expression of our personal, devotional prayer language because when we speak in tongues, we only edify ourselves. The people standing to the right and the left do not understand what we are saying and may be distracted, confused, or offended if we are loudly praying in the Spirit while they are trying to worship. I like to use the analogy of a house when explaining the need for expressing each gift in its appropriate context. In a house there are different rooms, and each room has its own function: we do not cook in the bedroom, shower in the kitchen, or sleep in the garage. The full and free expression of our personal prayer languages is a private matter between us and the Lord; it does not belong in the public rooms of the house.

The same is true when it comes to the gifts of the Spirit. A corporate gathering is not the place for personal edification that draws attention to the individual or distracts from the larger purpose of the meeting. If we want to walk in love as Christ did, we must lay down our individual rights, recognize that there is a place for everything, and ensure that we temper our expression of the gifts with love and respect. At the end of the day, love cares more about the experience of the others in the room than about personal freedom of expression. This is the model that we want to operate in:

> *If anyone speaks in a tongue, let there be two or at the most three, each in turn, and let one interpret. But if there is no interpreter, let him keep silent in church, and let him speak to himself and to God* (1 Corinthians 14:27-28).

The key phrase is found in the last verse. In a corporate setting we can speak to ourselves and to God; we can quietly commune with the Holy Spirit as long as we are not distracting or disturbing others.

This point is summarized at the end of Paul's teaching on the gifts of the Spirit: *"Therefore, brethren, desire earnestly to prophesy, and do not forbid to speak with tongues. Let all things be done decently and in order"* (1 Cor. 14:39-40). Paul makes two vital points in this passage. First, he says we must let *all* things be done. In other words, we must continue to love, pursue, and value the gifts of the Spirit in both private and public settings. He does not end there, however.

The second point is that the gifts must be expressed decently and in *order*. The edification of the corporate body and the orderliness of the meetings must be valued as much as the gifts of the Spirit are valued. Most ministries emphasize one of these points at the expense of the other. Some denominations will encourage everyone to run after the gifts and neglect decency and order, while others will maintain order at the expense of spiritual life. Only when we balance the two points will these gifts fulfill their intended role and actually serve, edify, and bless the Church.

We need to have this same heart posture when dealing with people from denominations that do not support the use of tongues. We want to love and serve our brothers and sisters, and we cannot do this if we are debating them. When I am invited somewhere and the leadership asks me not to speak in tongues, I respect the boundaries that they give me. I want to meet people where they are and not put a stumbling block in their way by insisting that they conform to my standards. (This is why Paul said that he became all things for all people in First Corinthians 9:22.) At the end of the day, debating this gift is a distraction that will not bear good fruit. I've never seen anyone really win a debate. We must have light and gentle spirits and display a willingness to love and bless our brothers and sisters even when they disagree with us.

ENDNOTE

1. We can experience this same resistance if we belong to a denomination that teaches against the gift of tongues. Listening to such teachings hardens our hearts and actually gives us faith to *resist* the Holy Spirit. Typically, believers who have never heard of the gift of tongues do not encounter resistance and receive their personal prayer language easily. We may need to repent on behalf of our denomination and break our agreement with teachings against the gifts and power of the Holy Spirit before we can receive the baptism of the Spirit.

Chapter 10

THERE IS MORE

About ten years ago I was gripped with the subject of the baptism of the Holy Spirit. I had already received the personal, devotional gift of tongues, and my life was filled with many other blessings and gifts of the Spirit. But deep within my heart, I knew that there had to be more. I was desperate for all that God would give to a human soul, and I knew that the "all" was more than the small manifestations of the gifts that I saw in my own life and the lives of those around me.

I read the Book of Acts, I read biographies of the great heroes of the faith, but it was only when I stumbled across the writings of John G. Lake—one of the fathers of the Pentecostal movement—that I began to find language for the cry of my heart. As I read his sermons, I discovered that the subject of the baptism of the Spirit and its impact on the Christian life has been greatly reduced over the last decades in the Church. We have treated this subject so lightly, yet this is the holiest thing that God can give to the human soul. Jesus suffered death on the cross, fought and defeated all the powers of hell, and finally ascended into

Heaven and received the Spirit from the Father so that He could pour it out on us; He understood the value of this gift.

On the Day of Pentecost, 120 believers were baptized in the Holy Spirit and they turned the world upside down. Today, the Church has millions of believers who are "baptized in the Spirit," and yet there is very little difference between them and the world. We have fallen so far short in our understanding of the baptism of the Spirit and what God longs to do in the souls of people. We cannot continue to believe that we possess all that God intended because we speak in tongues occasionally and have had a few experiences with manifestations of the Spirit. Simply reading the New Testament should convince us that there is a fundamental breakdown between what Jesus promised (and the early Church experienced) and what we experience today.

JOHN G. LAKE

I want to spend some time looking at the writings of John G. Lake. Lake arguably walked in some of the greatest levels of spiritual authority and power seen since the early Church. In his initial 18 months as a missionary in South Africa, Lake planted over 100 churches. At the end of his five years of ministry in that nation, he left behind 1250 preachers, 625 congregations, over 100,000 new converts, and countless testimonies of miraculous healings.[1] He then moved back to the United States—to Spokane, Washington—and set up a ministry school of healing. In its initial five years of existence, that school documented and recorded over 100,000 healings. The government actually investigated what had become known as the Healing Rooms, and gave this report: *"Rev. Lake, through divine healing, has made Spokane the healthiest city in the world, according to United States' statistics."*[2]

Here is an example of the power that Lake and his students were accustomed to seeing:

> Mrs. Constance Hoag, Puyallup, Washington, broke her kneecap. A section of the bone protruded through the flesh. She wrote requesting that ministers of the Healing Rooms lay their hands upon a handkerchief in faith and prayer and send it to her, in accordance with Acts 19:12. This was done. She applied the handkerchief to the knee and in about 15 minutes the pain had gone, and in an hour the bone had returned to place. A few days later she visited Spokane—well.[3]

This servant of God taught more on the baptism of the Holy Spirit than on any other subject. His own life was marked by an overwhelming desire to experience the fullness of the baptism of the Spirit, and his testimony of how God answered that hunger is powerful and provoking. John G. Lake was born in 1870. He was saved during his teenage years and began a successful ministry of healing in his twenties. This ministry continued for ten years, and Lake saw hundreds of people saved and healed. In a sermon delivered in 1921, Lake described that period of time and his hunger for more of the Holy Spirit:

> I ministered for ten years in the power of God. Hundreds and hundreds of people were healed by the power of God during this ten years, and I could feel the conscious flow of the Holy Spirit through my soul and my hands.
>
> But at the end of that ten years I believe I was the hungriest man for God that ever lived. There was such a hunger for God that as I left my offices in Chicago and walked down the street, my soul would break out, and I would cry, "Oh God!" I have had people stop

and look at me in wonder. It was the yearning passion of my soul, asking for God in a greater measure than I then knew. But my friends would say: "Mr. Lake, you have a beautiful baptism in the Holy Ghost." Yes, it was nice as far as it went, but it was not answering the cry of my heart. I was growing up into a larger understanding of God and my own soul's need. My soul was demanding a greater entrance into God, His love, presence and power.[4]

Lake began to earnestly fast and pray and cry out for the baptism of the Spirit. He spent nine months in intense intercession, begging God to baptize him in the way that Jesus' disciples had been baptized. One afternoon, a friend invited him to come and visit a woman who was suffering from severe rheumatism. While the friend conversed with the woman, Lake sat in a chair in the corner, crying out to God deep within his soul. Suddenly he was aware of the presence of God surrounding him, and he heard the Lord say, "I have heard your prayers, I have seen your tears. You are now baptized in the Holy Spirit."[5] At that moment, what felt like volts of electricity began to surge through his body. When he stretched out his hand toward the woman, his friend was thrown to the floor by the power released, and she was instantly healed and arose from her wheelchair. At this, his friend cried out, "Praise the Lord, John, Jesus has baptized you in the Holy Ghost!"[6]

It is true that after this encounter there was an increase in the anointing on Lake's ministry, especially in the realm of healing. He went through a season where he was able, simply by laying hands on a person, to tell which organ was diseased and how severely it was affected. He visited hospitals and accurately diagnosed numerous patients whom the doctors had given up on. Power was definitely a part of this baptism of the Spirit! But it was only a part. I want to share some of Lake's own writings related to the baptism of the Spirit. More than any other man in recent Church history, he grasped the heart of God behind the Day of Pentecost, and said yes to the highest vision of the Christian life.

> The outpouring of the Holy Ghost is the greatest event in Christian history—greater than the crucifixion, of greater import than the resurrection, greater than the ascension, greater than the glorification. It was the end and finality which the crucifixion, resurrection, and glorification sought to accomplish.
>
> If Jesus Christ had been crucified and there had been no resurrection, His death on the cross would have been without avail, insofar as the salvation of mankind is concerned. Or if He had risen from the grave in resurrection, failed to reach the throne of God and receive from the Father the gift of the Holy Ghost, the purpose for which He died and for which He arose would have been missed.
>
> There was no failure! Jesus went to the ultimate, the very throne and heart of God, and secured right out of the heavenly treasury the Almighty Spirit and poured Him forth upon the world in divine baptism; that is why we are here!
>
> ...in order to obtain this gift, Jesus Christ lived in the world, bled on the cross, entered into the darkness of death and hell and the grave, grappled with and strangled that accursed power, came forth again, and finally ascended to heaven in order to secure it for you and me. If there is anything under heaven that ought to command our reverence, our Holy reverence, our

reverence beyond anything else in the world, it surely is the subject of the Baptism of the Holy Ghost.[7]

Will you speak in tongues when you are baptized in the Holy Ghost? Yes, you will, but you will do an awful lot more than that, bless God. An awful lot more than that! You will speak with the soul of Jesus Christ. You will feel with the heart of the Son of God. Your heart will beat with a heavenly desire to bless the world, because it is the pulse of Jesus that is throbbing in your soul.[8]

Jesus went to heaven in order that the very treasury of the heart of the eternal God might be unlocked for your benefit, and that out of the very soul of the eternal God, the streams of His life and nature would possess you from the crown of your head to the soles of your feet, and that there would be just as much of the eternal God in your toe nails and in your brain as each are capable of containing. In other words, from the very soles of your feet to the last hair on the top of your head, every cell of your being, would be a residence of the Spirit of the living God. Man is made alive by God and with God, by the Spirit.[9]

The greatest manifestation of the Holy Ghost baptized life ever given to the world was not in the preaching of the apostles, it was not in the wonderful manifestations of God that took place at their hands, it was in the unselfishness manifested by the church. Think of it! Three thousand Holy Ghost baptized Christians in Jerusalem from the day of Pentecost onward who loved their neighbor's children as much as their own, who were so anxious for fear their brethren did not have enough to eat, that they sold their estates, and brought the money and laid it at the apostle's feet, and said: "Distribute it, carry the glow and the fire and the wonder of this divine salvation to the whole world." That showed what God had wrought in their hearts. Oh, I wish we could arrive at that place where this church was baptized in that degree of unselfishness.[10]

What Lake understood was that the baptism of the Spirit is about the fullness of God. We were created for communion; we were made to contain the glory of God. At salvation He places His Spirit in us, but when we are baptized, the Spirit who lives in us consumes us. We are immersed in who God is, and we manifest His life at every level: His power, His authority, and His sacrificial love. That is actually what it means to be baptized: total immersion. The baptism of the Spirit takes the reality of the life of God within and makes that reality experientially known to every part of our beings—body, soul, and spirit. Lake says it this way:

> ...beloved, we have not comprehended the greatness of God's intent. Not that we have not received the Spirit, but our lives have not been sufficiently surrendered to God. We must keep ascending right to the throne, right into the heart of God, right into the soul of the Glorified.[11]

This is the difference between the reality of the Holy Spirit *in* us and the Holy Spirit *upon* us. Again and again, Scripture testifies that there is more; there is a baptism of the Holy Spirit available to all believers. In fact, I believe that there are multiple baptisms. There are fresh encounters with the life of God that are released over the course of every believer's life. If you look at the New Testament Church and the lives of the disciples, it seems clear that there are multiple waves of anointing, power, and life that are received and experienced. As believers, we are invited to receive more and more of the Holy Spirit. *We are being baptized deeper into a Person, immersed in His life, His love, and His power.*

Reading the sermons of John G. Lake destroyed my spiritual complacency and I became consumed with desire for the fullness of all that God is willing to give His children. I am grateful for the baptism of the Spirit that I have received; I am grateful for the way that speaking in tongues has transformed my life—purifying my heart and mind, releasing revelation, strengthening my spirit, and overthrowing the schemes of the enemy—but I believe that there is more. As we engage the Holy Spirit through tongues and continue to press in for more, the Lord will usher us into greater measures of the fullness of God and the gifts of the Spirit. I believe that tongues is a gateway gift. The greatest signs and wonders, the most powerful healing and deliverance ministries, and the greatest harvest of souls will be released as the end-time Church reaps the fruit of ceaseless prayer in the Spirit.

I'm so desperate for this vision to possess the Church in America as well as all the nations of the earth. I believe that we must engage our prayer language like never before, knowing that it's this key that will unlock the door into the fullness of Christ in these last days. The truths contained in this book have revolutionized my spiritual life. I'm convinced they will do the same for a whole generation that is hungry to know and experience all that Jesus died for.

Set your heart on the journey, give yourself to it, and don't look up for the next decade!

ENDNOTES

1. *John G. Lake: His Life, His Sermons, His Boldness of Faith* (Fort Worth, TX: Kenneth Copeland Publications, 1994), xxv-xxvii.

2. Ibid., xxx.

3. Ibid., 320.

4. John G. Lake, "The Baptism of the Holy Ghost," in *John G. Lake: His Life, His Sermons, His Boldness of Faith* (Fort Worth, TX: Kenneth Copeland Publications, 1994), 483.

5. Gordon Lindsay, *John G. Lake: Apostle to Africa* (Dallas, TX: Christ For the Nations, Inc., 1987), 18.

6. Ibid., 19

7. Lake, "The Baptism of the Holy Ghost," 476.

8. Ibid., 484.

9. Ibid., 480.

10. Ibid., 490.

11. Ibid., 480.

About Corey Russell

Corey Russell currently serves on the senior leadership team of the International House of Prayer (IHOP-KC) as he has done for the last 11 years. Corey is the Director of the Forerunner Program at the International House of Prayer University (IHOPU), discipling and training young preachers and leaders. He travels nationally and internationally preaching on the themes of the Knowledge of God, Intercession, and the Forerunner Ministry. He resides in Kansas City with his wife, Dana, and their three daughters: Trinity, Mya, and Hadassah.

For booking and tracking with Corey's ministry:
www.coreyrussell.org.

Follow Corey on Twitter: @BrotherRussell

Follow Corey on Facebook: Official CoreyRussell

Contact: info@coreyrussell.org

Website:
www.coreyrussell.org
Facebook:
Official-CoreyRussell
YouTube:
officialcoreyrussell
Twitter:
@brotherrussell
Contact:
info@coreyrussell.org

Other Products *from* Corey Russell

The External Glory of
an Intercessor DVD

Ancient Paths CD

Days of Noah CD

Eyes Opened CD

Pursuit of the Holy

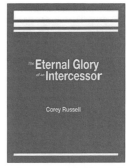

The External Glory of
an Intercessor
Study Guide

IN THE RIGHT HANDS, THIS BOOK WILL CHANGE LIVES!

Most of the people who need this message will not be looking for this book. To change their lives, you need to put a copy of this book in their hands.

> *But others (seeds) fell into good ground, and brought forth fruit, some a hundred-fold, some sixty-fold, some thirty-fold* (Matthew 13:8).

Our ministry is constantly seeking methods to find the good ground, the people who need this anointed message to change their lives. Will you help us reach these people?

> *Remember this—a farmer who plants only a few seeds will get a small crop. But the one who plants generously will get a generous crop* (2 Corinthians 9:6).

EXTEND THIS MINISTRY BY SOWING
3 BOOKS, 5 BOOKS, 10 BOOKS, OR MORE TODAY,
AND BECOME A LIFE CHANGER!

Thank you,

[signature]

Don Nori Sr., Founder
Destiny Image
Since 1982